THE MAGNIFICENT VISION

The Magnificent Vision

Seeing Yourself through the Eyes of Christ

Lloyd John Ogilvie

This Billy Graham Evangelistic Association special edition is published with permission from Servant Publications.

Servant Publications
Ann Arbor, Michigan

Dedication

To George Phelps,
whose vision and generosity model two great truths:
You can't outgive God;
what He guides, He provides.

Contents

Introduction

FREQUENTLY, *Reader's Digest* features an article entitled "My Most Unforgettable Character" about individuals who have had a great impact on others.

Who is the most unforgettable person you've ever met? I've met hundreds of them through the years, but if I were to write an article about the *most* unforgettable, one does stand out above the rest.

He's a laughing, loving, gloom-dispelling, life-affirming person. He loves profoundly, expresses non-stop joy, always seems at peace in the most troublesome situations. Not only that, this person has amazing patience, both with his friends and his self-appointed enemies. I'm always astounded by his kindness to people who mess up their lives, and I'm constantly surprised by his generosity. My friend is faithful and consistent. You can depend on his loyalty. There's a winsome gentleness about him, which seems to come from great inner strength. To top it all off, he's like a wind channel through whom power flows to anyone he meets.

You are probably wondering if there is anyone like that alive today. Yes, there is, and he's had a greater influence on my life than anyone else. I wish I could be like him, and he persistently reminds me that I can.

The most unforgettable character I've ever met is Jesus Christ. I purposely did not capitalize the pronouns in my description of my Lord in order to draw you into the stunning attributes of His character.

All this has been to establish the premise of this book: Christ can transplant His character into us. Impossible? Not when we see ourselves through the eyes of Christ. It's a magnificent vision that can come true. All of His character traits I listed can be ours! *Christ wants to make us like Himself!*

This magnificent vision of an amazing new you is captured by a figure of speech found in the New Testament which has an agrarian, almost archaic sound. This phrase seems strangely out-of-sync with the vocabularies of Christians living on the edge of the twenty-first century—in a technological society where one branch of science is preparing us for life in the galaxies, and another moves closer to producing a disease-free race of "ideal" human beings through the precise manipulation of human genes.

The figure of speech I refer to is "fruit of the Spirit." Far from being obsolete, the idea captured by this image transcends the temporal promises of the technologies I have just mentioned as a candle flame is transcended by the sun!

"Fruit of the Spirit" is the code name used by the apostle Paul for the spiritual "transplant" that takes place when the nature of Christ is formed and begins to grow in men and women, immortal creatures destined to live beyond time and space in resurrected bodies. In our own strength, it is absolutely impossible to live the kind of life Christ has called us to live. No amount of culture, education, or effort that is not empowered by His Spirit can produce Christian character.

Nothing is more tragic than a vision without the power to live it, and nothing more debilitating than discovering that the demands of becoming a *vital* Christian are too much for this genetic combination we call "self." We end up becoming people who are not authentic, prisoners of the falsehood that results when *Christian* becomes simply an adjective for a self-generated attempt to become like Christ without His indwelling power.

For most people, nothing is more discouraging than being charged from the pulpit every Sunday with the crimes of not loving enough, not being gentle or kind enough, not being patient enough, without having our rights read to us: Christ only requires from us what He places in us.

"Every time we say, 'I believe in the Holy Spirit,'" J.B. Phillips said, "we mean that we believe there is a living Lord able and willing to enter human personality and change it."

And so say I.

The implications of Paul's code name, fruit of the Spirit, are radical. They are also profoundly personal. Do you find it difficult to love? Would you like to experience the deep energy of pure joy? Do you desire the parched quality of your life to be replenished with the soft dew of peace? Do you need to be patient in some relationship? You possess an auxiliary power for all that and more. Within you exists a new control-power to halt the countdown of those debilitating emotional blast-offs, to find new courage to risk gentleness unafraid of being exploited, and to find reinforcement for diminishing self-control.

But wait, do you really *want* a new character?

Is it possible that we may have developed a spiritual narcissism—a fascination with what has been our experience, and what might keep us from new experiences of God's grace? Putting it another way, are we more committed to the god of our experience than to the fresh experience of God? The reason so many Christians find that they have such grave difficulty with their own human nature is that the fruit of the Spirit has not penetrated into their personalities.

We are going to examine the attributes of this new personality power as Paul listed them for the Galatian Christians:

The fruit of the Spirit is love, joy, peace, long-suffering, kindness, goodness, faithfulness, gentleness, self-control. Galatians 5:22-23

These characteristics are translated with slight variance in different versions of the Bible, but the essence remains the same.

Paul had a reason for confronting the Galatians with an inventory of what they could be in Christ. These first-century Christians had lost the freedom Paul introduced them to when he first helped them to know Christ and receive His Spirit. The Galatians were in a state of arrested spiritual development.

If ever a family of believers started out well, they did. They began their Christian life in the Spirit (Galatians 3:3). The Spirit taught them how to pray (4:6), and how to conduct themselves (5:13-16). They were set free from something many of us know about—the compulsiveness of an inherited religion with its rigidity, rules, and regulations.

But something happened. They were on the brink of regressing into the legalism of the ancient law. Life in Christ gave them the freedom to live what they had been taught by Paul, but some among them were now saying to new believers, "You have to become a Jew first, and fulfill all the obligations like we have, before you can go on to freedom in Christ." These were the Judaizers, those who said you had to become a Jew before you could become a Christian.

Can you imagine the suspense and tension in the Galatian congregation as Paul's letter was read? The message was patently clear. Your new life in Christ is not marked by ceremonies, he was saying, but by the celebration of love, joy, peace, patience, kindness, goodness, faithfulness, gentleness, and self-control. The hallmark graces of a new creature in Christ, he went on to say, are not governed by law. His strong implication was that they were not intended to make Christians split personalities either. "If we live in the Spirit," Paul wrote, "let us also walk in the Spirit" (Galatians 5:25).

Have you discovered any Galatian ghettos in the

churches of America—where God is seen as an awesome kind of cosmic policeman trying to catch us doing something wrong? Or where the Holy Spirit is seen as a private, separate specter of the Trinity, a mystical power that a person can tap into and receive what other believers do not have? Even the faith of persons who have recognized their sin, accepted God's forgiveness, and have made a commitment of as much as they know of themselves to as much as they know of God, can congeal into a set of creeds, ideas to be memorized, a subculture to support, denominational pride to maintain. In this type of situation, the whole dimension of the enabling power of the Spirit is missing. As in Galatia, the problem is compounded when dealing with newcomers to the faith.

To put it another way, consider the dilemma of the Christian parent. The question persists: How do we produce an honest, resolute, consistent, authentic Christian child?

Most of us have faced it in so many inadequate ways. We cajole, punish, barter, manipulate to somehow get children to do what they ought to do. We tell them about what it means to be an ideal Christian, but do we ever explain to them what we do with our failures, our vulnerabilities, and our inadequacies when we fail? The whole idea that we always have to be stronger, more adequate, more powerful, more convinced, and more faithful than our children is to tell them a lie and to keep them from experiencing the one power that will enable them to be like Jesus Christ.

The greatest gift we can give our children is to tell them what qualities we yearn to develop in them and to share with them the fact that Christian character cannot be earned. It cannot be inherited from Christian parents. Christian character is the result of Christ in us making us like Himself. He wants to take up His post–resurrection place in our hearts.

His presence there offers us an antidote to our struggles: love for our self-condemnation; joy for our discouragement; peace for our anxieties; patience for our pressures; kindness for our hostilities; goodness for our inconsistencies; faithfulness for our vacillations; gentleness for our judgmentalism; self-control for our turbulent desires for fulfillment.

For those of us who have been brought up in the church, we will find that it helps to avoid any association of the fruit of the Spirit with visual aids such as melons, apples, or pears. Paul's code word concerns itself primarily with the *process* of growth. Whether immersed in the soil, in the soft silent womb, or deep in the human spirit, all new births have something in common. Each is intricately programmed for growth, but all require the cooperation of forces and environments outside themselves to reach their potential. So does the miraculous growth process of the fruit of the Spirit.

In a world without penicillin, air conditioning, and modern plumbing, God's Son met human need head-on. He fleshed out a vision for us, in the simple graces of love, joy, peace, patience, kindness, goodness, faithfulness, gentleness, and self-control. After observing the quality of Christ's earthly, everyday relationships with the people of this world, John made this profound theological affirmation: "The Word became flesh, and dwelt among us, and we beheld His glory, the glory as of the only begotten of the Father, full of grace and truth" (John 1:14).

This book is about the continuing life of Jesus Christ in you and me. I invite you to do more than read it. Experience it. Most of all, catch a glimpse of the magnificent vision—the amazing new you as seen through the eyes of Christ.

ONE

The Second Half of the Blessing

Do you find it difficult to love? Would you like to experience the deep energy of pure joy? Do you want to move beyond images of God as a cosmic policeman, recording every infraction of the rules? If so, you may be ready to appreciate "the second half of the blessing."

E Lytle

The Second Half
of the Blessing

I S IT POSSIBLE we are cut from the same cloth, you and I? Strongwilled people, programmed to make it on our own even though we love and believe in Christ? It is difficult to admit our impotence and need, and yet, if we are honest, the time comes when we acknowledge that we are tired of the struggle. We wonder why our faith is so inadequate to help.

I offer you Christ's promise, "I have come that men may have life, and may have it in all its fullness" (John 10:10, NEB)—a two-part blessing.

We cannot have the second without the first. That must be said. But if we have the first without the second, our Christianity will continue to be nothing but a grim struggle.

THE FIRST HALF OF THE BLESSING

It is not my intention to play down the magnificent first half of the blessing—"I am come that you may have life." The Greek word used here is *zōē*, meaning "essential life." It is more than *bios* or *sōma* (physical life); or *psuchē* (thought and emotional life). Jesus speaks here of the quality of the eternal life He came to give.

He came to take us out of the warp of the power of sin and death. The charter of life He offers is in the kingdom of God, the liberating power is in His death on Calvary, and the defeat of death is in an open tomb. The purpose of Christ's incarnation was to do battle with the enemies of life and free us to live now—and forever. When we believe in Christ, we are ushered into a life over which death has no permanent power. Our sins are forgiven. We are released from self-condemnation. We are free to love ourselves as we are unreservedly loved by Him.

Remember when you first knew the Lord loved you? When you experienced the first half of His blessing? Jesus, who said of Himself, "I am the life," has given us the gift of life. Life beyond time. Forever. We did not deserve it. We could never earn it.

So what is wrong with being satisfied with that kind of blessing? "Sounds adequate to me," you say. And so it is to the majority of Christians.

But something happens as the years go by. We forget that the capacity for faith itself was a gift. We begin to act as if it were by some virtue of our own that we decided to become a Christian. The distance between us and Christ widens as we try to serve Him in our own strength.

Soon we substitute the carefully worded creeds and celebrations of the Christian year for a personal relationship. We pray and sing our way through Christmas, Good Friday, and Easter. The ho-hum of formalized familiarity sets in.

One by one, the old problems return like demons to the empty house. We struggle to be faithful and moral. We try to deal with life's problems. Christ is out there somewhere. We pray our prayers with little feeling of intimacy. The Lord who freed us from self-condemnation and ushered us into a deathless life becomes the awesome Holy Other of a formal I-Thou relationship. But we call Him in to help when our own management program breaks down, and then we wonder why He is so slow to respond to our imperious demands.

THE HALF-BLESSED CHRISTIAN

The problem of *the half-blessed Christian* is his or her lack of auxiliary power for life's struggles. The half-blessed Christian is befuddled and often immobilized by the perplexity of human nature. In "My Name Is Legion," Edward Sanford Martin said:

Within my earthly temple there's a crowd;
There's one of us that's humble, one that's proud,
There's one that's broken-hearted for his sins,
There's one that unrepentant sits and grins;
There's one that loves his neighbor as himself,
And one that cares for naught but fame and pelf.
From much corroding care I should be free
If I could once determine which is me.

Do you ever feel that way? Defeated over your own nature? Revolted by your thoughts, fantasies, actions, and reactions? Do you wonder how long you dare call yourself a Christian when there is so little of Christ's peace, power, and love in your life?

The apostle Paul's honesty and vulnerability about his own personal tensions is comforting. He shared his struggles. On one occasion, he turned a viscerally honest conversation he had with himself into part of his letter to the church at Rome. It is a letter few modern leaders would dare to write:

> I often find that I have the will to do good, but not the power. That is, I don't accomplish the good I set out to do, and the evil I don't really want to do I find I am always doing. Yet if I do things that I don't really want to do then it is not, I repeat, "I" who do them, but the sin which has made its home within me. When I come up against the Law I want to do good, but in practice I do evil. My conscious mind wholeheartedly endorses the Law, yet I observe an entirely different principle at work in my nature. This is in continual conflict with my conscious attitude, and makes me an unwilling prisoner to the law of sin and death. In my mind I am God's willing servant, but in my own nature I am bound fast, as I say, to the law of sin and death. It is an agonizing situation, and who on earth can set me free from the clutches of my own sinful nature? **Romans 7:18-24, Phillips**

In classical simplicity Paul has described the downside of the half-blessed life. He has polarized the difference between having religion and having a deep relationship with the indwelling Christ. Charles Kingsley must have arrived at this same dark intersection. "What I want is not to possess a religion," he said, "but to have a religion that shall possess me." And John Oxenham in "Credo":

> Not what, but *Whom*, I do believe,
> That, in my darkest hour of need,
> Hath comfort that no mortal creed
> To mortal man may give.
> Not what, but *Whom!*

It is a very special gift from the Lord when we experience a crisis in the inadequacy of the "what" of religion, and want the "Whom" of dynamic faith.

A moment ago I interrupted the apostle Paul as he was asking: "Who on earth can set me free from the clutches of my own sinful nature?" He answers his own question: "I thank God there is a way out through Jesus Christ our Lord. No condemnation now hangs over the head of those who are in Jesus Christ. For the new spiritual principle of life in Christ lifts me out of the old vicious circle of sin and death" (Romans 7:25-8:2, Phillips).

I discovered this after my first year in the ministry. I was forced to face one of the most disturbing truths about leadership—we can lead others only so far as we have gone ourselves. *Nothing can happen through us which has not happened to us.* Obviously, what my people needed had not happened to me. Their great need was for power to live the Christian life that I was preaching.

The Lord had allowed the crisis of my emptiness to bring me to the astounding realization that I was living with only half a blessing. During the solitude and quiet of a study leave, as I was preparing the next year's sermons, my prayers for my people forced me to admit that

I had preached only half the gospel.

Certainly I was preaching Christ as the crucified and resurrected Lord of all life. My sermons were packed with what Christ had done *for* us, or what He could do *with* us as our companion and friend. But, inadvertently, I had avoided His promise of what He could do *in* us. I fell to my knees and asked for help.

I will never forget what happened. As I resumed my study, I was guided to the verse we've been considering, John 10:10. Christ's words exploded with a freshness. It was as if I had never heard Him before: "I am come that they might have life, and that they might have it more abundantly."

A TWO-DIMENSIONAL PROMISE

What thundered with clarity was that I had just read a two-dimensional promise—first life, and then abundant life. The first part dealt with what the Lord came to do. The second part dealt with what He comes to do now.

I was face to face with the truth implicit in Paul's code name. It was a truth I had never dealt with before. I had preached the life of Christ and taught that the Christian life was the identification with Christ's Cross for our forgiveness, His Resurrection for our victory over death, and His living presence for the guidance of our daily lives. Now the Lord seemed to be saying, "That's only half the blessing. Press on!"

I checked the meaning of *abundant* life in the original Greek—"fullness, superabundance, overflowing, limitless." Those adjectives did not describe my life, but I desperately wanted them to. Suddenly, I felt the tumultuous excitement of a potential breakthrough to new power.

In rapid-fire order, verses of Scripture I had known and memorized were screened on the monitor of my memory. I saw that all of them had something in common. They all revolved around the powerful preposition *in*. The Lord had said that He would be *with* us. But He also promised that He would be *in* us. "Abide in Me, and I in you... for without Me you can do nothing" (John 15:4-5).

And suddenly there it was. If life is Christ, the abundant life must be more of Him! To be in Christ as believer, disciple, and a loved, forgiven person is one thing. To have Christ in us as motivator, enabler, and transformer of personality is something more. Much more. I knew then what Paul meant when he told the Colossians: "The mystery which has been hidden from ages and from generations, but now has been revealed to His saints. To them God willed to make known what are the riches of the glory of this mystery... which is Christ in you, the hope of glory" (Colossians 1:26-27).

Think of it! Our minds, emotions, and wills are meant to be the post-resurrection home of the immanent, intimate, indwelling Lord!

Closely linked to this discovery was another—the Holy Spirit and the living Spirit of Christ are one. When Christ promised the gift or comfort of the Holy Spirit (John 14:16-17), He quickly identified Himself with the Spirit. "I will come to you," He said. "A little while longer and the world will see Me no more, but you will see Me. Because I live, you will live also" (John 14:18-19).

Talk about abundant life! Christ is the revelation of God and the personification of the Holy Spirit. That same Spirit who created all—who dwelt in Christ to save us—that same Spirit is with us now as indwelling Lord. He is with us to give us faith to accept what He did for us as the Messiah, and to accept all He can do through us by forming the fruit of the Spirit—His nature—in us. "At that day you will know that I am in my Father, and you in me, and I in you" (John 14:20).

It was 1957. Eight years before, the Lord had created the sense of need, given me the gift of faith, and had become my Savior. Then He waited patiently for me to run out of my own resources in an effort to live the new life in Him. All alone with Him that summer afternoon at the end of my weary journey of self-propelled discipleship, I invited Him to fill me with His Spirit. I have never been the same since.

Our commitment to Christ is only a beginning. The Lord longs to give us more and more. Remember when He said, "For whoever has, to him more will be given, and he will have abundance; but whoever does not have, even what he has will be taken away from him" (Matthew 13:12). That startling statement is a special assurance to half-blessed Christians. We have the blessing of initial faith. We are now ready to receive in abundance.

The second half of the blessing is the abundance of Christ Himself. It is the promise of the fruit of the Spirit. Not what, but Whom. Not then, but now. Not near, but here. Not only Christ *with* us, but Christ *in* us. "Christ in you, the hope of glory."

If the first half of our blessing is *eternal* life, the second half is *abundant* life. To be in Christ is one thing. To have Christ in us is sublimely more wonderful! Now we are ready to actually see the magnificent vision of what we can be when filled with the fruit of the Spirit.

TWO

Extraordinary Love

The kind of love Jesus models is astonishing, so unlike our meager efforts to tolerate difficult people or to be nice to people who are not nice to us. More astonishing still, Christ enables us to overcome our resentment and our too-easily injured pride so we can practice His extraordinary love.

Extraordinary Love

"**O**H, HE'S very ordinary. And what's more, he's ordinary by choice!"

What a description of a "half-the-stops-out" person! Ordinary by choice! I can't imagine a more demeaning verdict.

Abraham Lincoln said, "The Lord prefers common-looking people, that is the reason He makes so many of them." But God has made no ordinary people. We become ordinary by our own choice not to be great people. Each of us is special, unique.

Jesus Christ came to reveal extraordinary living. He called a new breed of humanity to live in Him and allow Him to live in them. The extraordinary life consists in receiving and communicating extraordinary love: Christ's love as He lived it; His love in us; and our love for others motivated by Him.

It is important to note that the word *fruit* in Paul's code name is not pluralized by him. He does not say: "The fruits of the Spirit *are....*" To do so would seem to destroy the unity of the image he has chosen to illustrate the power of Christ's life force within us. The word *fruit* is singular for a second reason. It represents the one and only source from which Christlike character can flow—the Spirit of Christ Himself.

The fruit of the Spirit is love.

Paul selected a Greek word for "love" that is generally used to express divine love as distinct from human love or friendship. This divine dimension of extraordinary love will affect all loves, but we are called to be containers and transmitters of God's love to the world. The life and message of Christ reveals it; His presence in us elevates us beyond the ordinary to experience and express it. This love, which is a fruit of His dwelling within us, is unmerited, lived on the millionth mile, and impossible for us on our own.

The extraordinary love Jesus requires in the Sermon on the Mount is what He inspires when He comes to make His home in us. Jesus expressed this love throughout His life, and His Spirit returned at Pentecost to make such love possible in the extraordinary lovers who came to be known as the Christians.

IMPOSSIBLE LOVE?

The disciples would have been astonished when they first heard about this divine dimension of love. It is not the kind of love that comes naturally for people. It is the kind of love that gives us resiliency in our resentment and releases others from recrimination. The love Jesus taught is more than family affection (*storgē*); far more than the passion of human love (*erōs*); infinitely more than warm friendship (*philia*). Christ's love is unconquerable acceptance and benevolence for people, regardless of what they do or who they are.

The Sermon on the Mount confronts us with the essential nature of this love. It is unmotivated. Nothing that the recipient does, or refuses to do, stirs its sublime power. Just as God's love for us in Christ was not motivated by our accomplishments or adequacy, so, too, the fruit of the Spirit in us is a love that is not motivated by the person who needs it. That's what makes it extraordinary! It comes from God. His Spirit in us is the only motivation. Matthew 5:38-48 is our charter, offering the secret of love for people we resent and those who have become our enemies. Read it again in preparation for our consideration of the gift of unmotivated love we want to claim in this chapter.

I once talked to a man who was being eaten alive by his resentments. In an hour's conversation, he said twenty times directly or indirectly, that he was resentful. I counted! He had come to see me about a growing sense of anxiety. The cause became obvious: he had turned his resentments inward on himself. Because he said he was a Christian, he had forbidden himself ever to get angry. But he was angry—at people, at life in general, and, in a way, at God. The virus of resentment had attacked his soul. And resentment, like revenge, is not sweet. It is poisonous!

How about you? Do you ever feel put upon, misused, harmed, misunderstood, taken for granted? How do you handle it when people do or say things which hurt or hinder you? Listen to your own words. "I resent that!" "I resent what he does!" "I resent the way you relate to me!"

In this passage from the Sermon on the Mount, Jesus reiterates the *lex talionis* or ordinary love. "You have heard that it was said, 'An eye for an eye and a tooth for a tooth'" (Matthew 5:38). This law was based on Exodus 21:23-24: "You shall give life for life, eye for eye, tooth for tooth, hand for hand, foot for foot, burn for burn, wound for wound, stripe for stripe." This may seem harsh, but it actually represented a step toward mercy. In the ancient world, it was common for an injured person to wipe out the whole tribe of the person who had harmed or maligned him. This law of Moses went beyond that to an exact *quid pro quo*. Later, even that became refined by the development of the *Baba Kamma* in which the courts decided the payment of money for injury.

But here is Jesus with an alarming, astounding challenge. He calls for no retaliation at all! "But I tell you not to resist an evil person" (v. 39). That means, "Don't get involved in active retaliation against people who do evil toward you." He then makes it very specific in four kinds of insults which cause us to be resentful.

The first deals with insults to our dignity. "But whoever slaps you on your right cheek, turn the other to him also." A right-handed person standing in front of another person would have to use the back of his or her hand to strike the blow. According to rabbinic law, to hit a person with the back of the hand was twice as insulting as to hit him or her with the flat of the hand.

The insults we suffer come not so much from the flat of the hand as from the words flatly spoken to or about us. And Jesus says offer the other cheek. Now we see why we need the unmotivated quality of extraordinary love.

What insults linger in your memory? When things people have said drift back to us through the gossip network, we feel anger and resentment. We want to get back at the person, return the volley. We hurt.

THE POWER TO FORGIVE

We need the fruit of love when forgiveness is required. Only a fresh experience of Christ's forgiveness can enable us to forgive and not return a retributive insult. Or we say, "I'll forgive, but I won't forget!" That is just another way of saying that we will not forgive. Only Christ can help us fulfill Paul's challenge, "Be kind to one another, tenderhearted, forgiving one another, as God in Christ forgave you" (Ephesians 4:32). Forgiveness was so crucial to the Master that it was the only dimension of the Lord's Prayer that He reiterated for emphasis. "If you forgive men their trespasses, your heavenly Father will also forgive you. But if you do not forgive men their trespasses, neither will your Father forgive your trespasses" (Matthew 6:14-15).

The parable of the unmerciful servant nails that down tighter than we would like. A king wanted to settle his accounts with debtors. One owed him ten thousand talents. A talent was worth about one thousand dollars. Ten million dollars! What a debt. We are shocked. The debtor could not possibly pay. The king followed the law of the land: the servant and his family were sentenced to slavery. And yet, when the man begged the king for mercy, the debt was forgiven. We would expect that servant to be the most magnanimous man alive after that.

Instead, immediately he went to find one of his debtors who owed him one hundred denarii—twenty dollars at most. He demanded payment. What a contrast. Twenty dollars in contrast to ten million! When the servant's debtor could not pay, he took him by the throat, throttled him, and threw him into prison.

The point of Jesus' story is not what the king's servant did before his forgiveness, it was what he did afterward. But news like that travels fast. It got back to the king who revoked his previous forgiveness and handed the servant over, not just to prison, but to the torturers.

The conclusion of the parable is frightening. We cannot tear it from our Bibles. Jesus said, "So My heavenly Father also will do to you if each of you, from his heart, does not forgive his brother his trespasses" (Matthew 18:35). That shakes us in our boots! The word *heart* is the key. Only the fruit of love, Christ's love, can give us the power to forgive from our hearts. When our hearts are His home, He does the forgiving through us. Alexander Pope was right: "To err is human, to forgive divine."

FREED FROM DEFENSIVENESS

Next, Jesus focuses on the invasion of a person's rights. "If any one wants to sue you and take away your tunic, let him have your cloak also" (Matthew 5:40). The coat, or tunic as other translations render it, was a *chitōn*, a long inner garment of cotton or linen. Most people had several of these. The cloak was more valuable: it was a great, blanket-like garment worn as outer clothing by day and used as a blanket by night. Ancient Hebrew law protected this possession. "If you ever take your neighbor's garment as a pledge, you shall restore it to him before the sun goes down. For that is his only covering, it is his garment for his skin. What will he sleep in?" (Exodus 22:26-27).

To sue a man for his tunic was to take him to court for all he had. It is like saying, "I'll sue you right down to the clothes on your back!" or, "I'll take you for everything you've got!" When someone does that, Jesus says, offer him your cloak also. Give him your pledge. Tell him that you want to get to the bottom of his grievances and settle the matter. He is calling for freedom from defensiveness. When our security is in Him, we can look at accusations honestly. We are liberated to admit where we have failed and be graciously open where we have not. What a wonderful way to live!

The fruit of love is communicated in a desire to see things as they are. Fortified by the power of such love, we can say to people who accuse us, "Listen, you feel you have a right to this because of what you think I've done to you. I want to hear you out, and I promise to seek your forgiveness if, after the whole matter is exposed, I have acted wrongly." Or we can say, "You have a grievance against me. I give you my pledge that I want to know what you perceive I've done and settle the matter." In other words, "If I've hurt you, I want to know how. You have a right to your feelings. I want to know what I might have done." No ordinary love, that!

I have great admiration for the founders of the Christian Legal Society, an organization which seeks to help Christians in the negotiation of conflicts which otherwise could end up in long and costly court battles.

My esteemed friend Robert Toms, one of the nation's top attorneys, is one of the founders. Along with others, he has fleshed out Jesus' admonition, "Agree with your adversary quickly, while you are on your way with him, lest your adversary deliver you to the judge" (Matthew 5:25). These Christian lawyers help people demonstrate the essence of extraordinary love in conflicts. People are encouraged to admit that there are two sides to every issue, and are helped to enter into prayerful negotiation, transforming lose-lose situations into win-win resolutions. The most formidable challenge is always to set people free of defensiveness.

Christ in us can free us of that truncated vision. He gives us double vision to look at ourselves and the other person. Resentment over the invasion of our rights is cured by a growing sense of righteousness with the Lord.

OUR TOO-EASILY INJURED PRIDE

But what about our pride? Jesus goes on to confront injuries to our pride. He does that with an example familiar to all His listeners in saying that if anyone forces you to go one mile, you should go with him two miles (Matthew 5:41). In Jesus' time, a Roman soldier could lay his sword on the shoulder of any Jew and make him carry a load like a beast of burden. It was an excruciating insult. Roman roads were marked off in one-mile sections. It was as if Jesus was saying, "If a Roman compels you to go a mile, keep the load on your back and astound him by going a second mile." The Greek word *aggareuein* (compel), from the word *aggareus*, actually came from the Persian postal service word meaning "courier." The Persian couriers could press people or their property into their service at will. Eventually, the word came to mean the power of an occupying army to conscript a conquered people into the most menial tasks.

When we combine this statement of Jesus' with His admonitions about forgiveness to Peter, we realize that He meant not only the second mile, but the millionth mile of living. The reluctant disciple wanted to set limits on forgiveness: "Up to seven times?" The Master's immediate reply was a Hebraism which meant without limits, "I do not say to you, up to seven times, but up to seventy times seven" (Matthew 18:22). The same is true when our pride is injured by what people do to us.

We feel resentment when people ask us to do something that we think is beneath us because we are over-qualified, or when they neglect to ask us to do something for which we are eminently qualified. Our feelings are out-of-sorts too much of the time. The sights and oversights rankle us. We stew in our own emotional juices, all because our security is misplaced. There is no limit to the good we can do when we do not care who gets the glory and recognition. But that takes more than ordinary love.

The fourth thing Jesus confronts is our reactions to intrusions on our privacy. The three most important human commodities we have are time, experience, and money. We all feel resentment when people demand our time when it is not convenient or when we are under pressure. They impose on us as if they were the only people alive and all we have to do is to be with them. Also, we resent people who refuse to do their own homework and leech on our learning and experience, hammered out in years of hard work. We all feel mixed reactions when we are assailed by poachers, beggars, and friends who want money we have worked hard to earn. Once I was accosted by a man on the street who asked me for a dollar—not for a cup of coffee, but for a beer! Another person on the street said what we all feel at times, "I don't know why these people don't work for a living like the rest of us." But most disturbing to us are our friends and relatives who never become independent and are constantly on our doorstep wanting us to support their irresponsibility.

THE MINISTRY OF COMPASSION

Then we hear Jesus' call for extraordinary giving as an expression of love. "Give to him who asks you and from him who wants to borrow from you do not turn away" (Matthew 5:42). The more I ponder that, the more dependent I am on the Lord to live it. He reminds me that all that I have and am is His gift. Without Him I could not breathe a breath, think a thought, write a sentence, preach a message, earn a dime, or develop my life. All that I have is from Him to be given away lavishly. We often hear the old shibboleth, "You can't take it with you." Wrong! We will take our souls with us into eternity. What we have done with outer resources will dramatically affect the inner person that death cannot destroy. The parable of the rich man and Lazarus drives that frightening point closer to home than we like.

Most people do not need the material things we can give or lend, but rather they need our love. That is the deeper implication of Jesus' admonition. It is easy to give a handout and hope we will never see the person again. Instead of a dollar for a beer for the man on the street, it took three dollars for a meal and hours of my time, and the members of Alcoholics Anonymous in my church, to set the man free of his compulsive alcoholism by helping him experience Christ's love and forgiveness.

People who are habitually in need of money really need help to get on their feet. They require prolonged times of counseling and an introduction to the Savior. That means not just our time, but ourselves. I could not take the pressures of human need in Los Angeles and the burdens of people who come to town seeking help as a result of our national television ministry, if it were not for the team of extraordinary lovers in my church, members who have discovered that to be in Christ is to be in ministry. No pastor can see all the people who need him. He was never meant to. The ministry of compassion is given to all the congregation.

To be free to give ourselves away is the fruit of Christ the Vine. When we are branches attached to the unlimited source of love, we are never alone or without an adequate flow of healing grace for others.

There is a difference between "getting even" and "even getting." One is the way of resentment; the other the way of release. Getting even is normal life stretched to the breaking point and severed. Even getting is proportionate inflow and outgo—we are never asked to give more than we have received. We are channels, not holding tanks, of love. If we get to a place where the resources have run out, we need to check our connection to the vine. No root, no fruit!

THE FOUR STEPS OF LOVING

Jesus goes on in the Sermon on the Mount to give us the specific steps of communicating extraordinary love. He does it in contrast to teaching current at the time: "You shall love your neighbor and hate your enemy." His startling challenge was, "*Love* your enemies, *bless* those who curse you, *do good* to those who hate you, and *pray* for those who spitefully use you and persecute you" (Matthew 5:44). The key to expressing that kind of love is in the experience of the family characteristic of God's character shared with His children: "That you may be sons of your Father who is in heaven" (Matthew 5:45). Jesus tells us that we can be like God in the communication of His love. I would like to suggest a reordering of the active verbs *love, bless, do good,* and *pray* in a progression that works for me:

pray
love
bless
do good

It is consistent with the Lord's total message and gives us some specific steps to take in being extraordinary lovers.

Start with prayer. Talk to the Lord about the person you find it difficult to love; ask the Lord to show you the deeper reason. In conversation, allow Him to give you His perspective on the person and his or her hidden needs you may not have perceived. In the quiet, picture the person as loved by Christ and filled with his Spirit. Claim that it will be so!

Next, ask for the gift of love for that person. Tell the Lord that you cannot love him or her by yourself. Ask for a special infilling of giving and forgiving love that only the Lord can provide.

Now, put that into words to the person. To bless is to belong and to be beloved. We are beloved by God and so can bless others. Most people need to hear in words what the Lord has helped us to experience. Answer this question: What could I say that would help that person to know I am for him or her, that nothing can change my attitude? People so desperately need affirmation and encouragement.

Lastly, as a companion to words of love, "do good" to the person. What is the loving act that will make our words believable? The Lord will help us discern what that is. Love is what we do along with what we say.

Whenever I follow these simple, decisive steps, the fruit of love changes me and then the relationship. And I discover what Jesus meant when He concluded this section of the Sermon on the Mount. "Therefore you shall be perfect, just as your Father in heaven is perfect" (Matthew 5:48). The word for "perfect" in Greek is *teleios,* from *telos,* meaning "purpose, end, goal." The purpose of our lives is to be loved and to love. *Living is for loving.*

No one can read or digest Jesus' explanation of extraordinary love without exclaiming, "That's impossible!"

The response is exactly what Jesus expects and wants. If we could do it by ourselves, we would not need the precious fruit of His love. That leaves us with this perturbing question, "What are we attempting in loving others that we could never pull off without the indwelling power of the Lord's love?" *We were never meant to be ordinary.* Offering others unmerited love is the authentic hallmark of a Spirit-filled Christian.

THREE

Non-Stop Joy

Why are there so many dogged, joyless, do-it-yourself Christians? Are we missing something essential? Joy is for the journey, especially for the most difficult parts of it, not just for the reflective moments after the storm.

Non-Stop Joy

JOY HAS NOTHING TO DO WITH gush or ho-ho jolliness. It is more than happiness. It is impervious to difficult situations and impossible people. Joy is an outward expression of grace, God's unmerited love. The Greek word for "grace" is *charis* and the word for "joy" is *chara*. They both come from the same root.

Joy is the second character trait awaiting development in us, listed under Paul's code name *fruit*.

The fruit of the Spirit is joy.

I want to tackle a disturbing question. Why are there so many dogged, joyless, do-it-yourself Christians? We see them everywhere. Some experience sporadic, fleeting moments of joy, but they are not lasting or consistent. Allow me to suggest a possible answer that has been growing to conviction-sized proportions in my mind.

Joy is the result of being loved by God. When His undeserved grace and forgiveness penetrate through the thick layers of self-doubt and self-negation, we begin to feel the surge of joy. Self-esteem and joy go together. We can joyously exclaim, "I'm glad I'm me!" That's not easy for most Christians. We find it difficult to let God love us and change our demeaning self-image. It takes a constant reminder of how much God loves us. The Cross alone can balance the scales weighted with self-condemnation.

WHY SO MANY JOYLESS CHRISTIANS?

But why is it that Christians who know about the grace of God repeatedly still miss the joy? There are several reasons; each presses us deeper into an understanding of true joy.

First, there can be no joy without Christ living in us. His promises about joy are all connected to realizing a profound intimacy with Him. Like love, joy flows from the vine into the branch. When we abide in Him and He in us, we know joy. In John 15, Jesus took great care to explain His "I Am" assertion: that He was the true vine from whom our spiritual vitality flows. Right after that He said, "These things I have spoken to you, that joy may remain in you, and that your joy may be full" (John 15:11). R. Leonard Small's now classic statement summarizes the promise: "Joy is the standard that flies on the battlements of the heart when the King is in residence." Jesus Christ Himself is our joy!

Second, many people miss the joy because they don't expect to experience it in the midst of difficulties. In John 16, Christ told us that we would know sorrow and disappointment, but that it would be a prelude to experiencing new joy. He used the image of a woman in childbirth. The birth process is not easy; the hopes and dreams which grow in us are often painful. But because of the joy of the birth, the anguish is soon forgotten. "Therefore you now have sorrow, but I will see you again and your heart will rejoice and your joy no one will take from you... most assuredly I say to you, whatever you ask the Father in My name He will give you. Until now you have asked nothing in My name. Ask, and you will receive, that your joy may be full" (John 16:22-24).

The conclusion of Jesus' message there in the upper room gives the secret source of His joy. His honest statement about reality is coupled with the assurance of His victory over evil and death. He faced the Cross with this assurance: "Yet I am not alone, because the Father is with me" (v. 32). Then He gave the disciples the liberating legacy for joy. "These things I have spoken to you, that in Me you may have peace. In the world you will have tribulation; but be of good cheer, I have overcome the world" (v. 33).

Joy is not something we know only when everything is smooth and easy. It is not spiritual ecstasy when all our problems are solved. Rather, joy is the special fruit of the indwelling Christ in the actual experience of problems. The reason so many Christians miss the joy is that they keep waiting for a time when life's complications will be resolved. We think of joy as compensation for working things out *for* the Lord. Instead, true joy is His companionship during the battle, not only after the battle. Many of us feel we have no right to feel joyous as long as we are not perfect, still have areas in which we need to grow, and continue to face unresolved tensions. But joy is for the journey, not just for the reflective moments after the journey.

The essential difference between happiness and joy is

that happiness is usually circumstantial and situational. The root of the meaning of *happiness* is *hap,* meaning "chance"; the root of joy is changeless love.

When the King is in residence we are able to fight life's battles with joy. We become "overcomers." Troublesome people and frustrating situations, pressures and challenges, disappointments and grief, heartache and sorrow will all be infused with joy, because we know that the Lord will use them all for our growth and His glory.

A journalist caught the meaning of joy in Pope John Paul II. He said Pope John Paul seemed to always convey an almost tangible sense of strength and extraordinary low-burning joy, joy in adversities endured... in being a Christian and in being human.

JOY AND HONESTY

Many of us deny our humanity in our search for joy. Life is run on two tracks, one of bold beliefs and the other of life's difficulties. A Spirit-filled Christian can dare to bring the two together. We can be honest with ourselves and the Lord about what we are going through and feeling. Surrender is the key. When we turn our real world over to our Lord and know that He will work everything together for good, the fruit of joy is expressed in our character and countenance.

When we block the Lord from meeting our real needs, thinking we should be responsible to work those out ourselves, we checkmate Him from reaching us where we need Him most desperately! That has been difficult for me to learn. There is still that lingering misconception that if I were more faithful and obedient, there would be no pressing needs in my life.

Once I went through a confrontation with a person I love very much. He had some things to say that hurt deeply. Afterwards, I had a bad case of the "if onlys." Do you ever get them? As long as I dealt with my feelings defensively, there was no joy. Then I was brought to my knees in my heart again. "Lord, what can I learn from this? What are you trying to tell me? I hurt, Lord, and need you very much!" Joy flooded my heart. The situation was not resolved completely, but joy returned. I knew that the One who gives each day would show the way. There were things I needed to do and say to correct the problem, but I was able to do them with joy.

The same thing has happened to me all through my life and ministry. Joy was given me as a fruit of the Spirit years ago. The sowing and harvesting of that gift have usually come in the midst of stretching challenges and soul-sized opportunities.

I write this with you in mind. Perhaps you are going through something right now that is painful and excruciating. Most of us are. There will always be problems; that is life. But there will also be more than adequate strength; that is joy. Don't wait until the crisis is over to allow yourself the delicious fruit of joy. True joy is but a prayer of surrender away. Get in touch with where you are hurting and hoping. That will be the focus of a new joy. When your energy and resources are diminished, you can count on the Lord's joy to fuel and reinforce your human spirit in all possible (and impossible!) situations. Praise God for crises. They are fresh opportunities to experience joy.

"I WILL JOY—REGARDLESS"

In preparation for writing this chapter, I did a comprehensive review of the word joy in Scripture. It is almost always experienced in the context of some difficulty or in reflection on what the Lord had made of the raw material of discouragement. What the Lord will do, is doing, and has done, is our joy.

The prayer of Habakkuk has become one of my favorites. It reminds us that the fruit of joy is produced when other harvests are barren.

> Though the fig tree may not blossom,
>   nor fruit be on the vines,
> though the labor of the olive may fail
>   and the fields yield no food;
> though the flock be cut off from the fold,
>   and there be no herd in the stalls—
> yet I will rejoice in the Lord,
>   I will joy in the God of my salvation.
> The Lord God is my strength;
>   He makes my feet like deer's feet,
>   And He will make me walk on my high hills.
>
> **Habakkuk 3:17-19**

Note how the word *joy* is used as part of the future verb form of the Hebrew word. Not, "I will have joy," but, "I will joy"! It actually means "I will spin about with delight and adoration." A pirouette of praise. A noun becomes a verb for daily living. Not a bad commitment for all of life, "I will joy—regardless."

Another verse that gives us the distilled meaning of joy is Acts 13:52, "And the disciples were filled with joy and the Holy Spirit." They had every reason not to be.

They had just lived through a hard time of rejection and persecution in Antioch of Pisidia. Note what happened just before the disciples experienced the fresh flush of joy in the Holy Spirit. "The Jews stirred up the devout women and the chief men of the city, raised up persecution against Paul and Barnabas, and expelled them from their region. But they shook off the dust from their feet against them, and came to Iconium" (vss. 50-51).

I like that. Joy did not depend on human success, the approval of people, or having everything go right. The disciples could press on to the next challenge. The Holy Spirit gave them joy for the next steps of the strategy. Paul is always very clear about the source of joy. It is inspired by the Holy Spirit (1 Thessalonians 1:6).

But there is a further reason some Christians miss the joy. True joy is a part of God's nature that He wants to share with His children. It is a family characteristic. What gives God joy is the source of our joy. In fact, there is no lasting joy until we are partners with God in what He is doing in the world. According to the parabolic teaching of Jesus, God experiences joy whenever we join Him in concern for the lonely and the lost. The old gospel song says, "If you want joy, real joy, let Jesus come into your heart." That is fine as far as it goes. We should also sing, "If you want to keep joy, real joy, let Jesus flow out of your heart to others."

THE LOST AND FOUND DEPARTMENT

In the parables of the lost son, the sheep, and the coin, Jesus tells us that God and the whole company of heaven experience sublime joy whenever the lost are found. The elder brother missed sharing that joy. The shepherd who left the ninety-nine sheep in search of the one lost sheep shared the heart of God when he recovered the wandering one. And the woman who would not give up until she had found the lost coin tasted the joy of heaven when she found it. The "lost and found" department of heaven is always open.

God's joy is the result of love received. He knows no greater joy than when we let Him love us. And our joy, as sons and daughters of our heavenly Father, is a byproduct of allowing Him to love others through us. A personal note: The only greater joy for me than becoming a Christian has been helping other people live forever by introducing them to Christ and salvation. Joy breaks forth in inner delight when I have been given the privilege of leading another person to the Lord and to the great adventure of life in the Lord. Joy becomes a lasting fruit when I am free to love and care, give and forgive, listen to and hope for people.

Whenever Christians tell me they have lost the joy they once had, my first question is, "When was the last time you helped someone meet Christ?" How would you answer that? Who is alive in Christ because of you?

The more I study the parable of the talents in Matthew 25:14-30, the more convinced I become that Jesus was talking about reproducing our faith, enabling others to know Him. He taught the parable at the end of His ministry. He knew that He was going away, the Cross was ahead, and He would be back.

The parable of the talents was based on a custom of the time. Local provincial leaders deployed by the Roman Empire were often called back to Rome. While they were gone, they entrusted their properties and investments to subordinates. Jesus built on the familiar to teach an unfamiliar, and very surprising, truth. We will get the full impact if we identify the "man" going away on a journey with the Lord Himself, and the servants with the disciples and with us.

You know the story. One was given one talent, another two, and the other five. Remember, a talent was worth about a thousand dollars. Whether $1,000, $2,000 or $5,000, each was given a great sum to invest. Both the two- and five-talent servants doubled their investment. The one-talent servant was afraid of losing what he had and buried his talent in the ground.

Inevitably, the time of accounting came. Note that the two- and five-talent servants received accolades for the multiplication of their investment and were invited to a very special privilege—the *joy* of the master. The one-talent servant said, "I was afraid, and I went and hid your talent in the ground." The punishment for that was severe. "Therefore take the talent from him," the master said, "and give it to him who has the ten talents. For to every one who has, more will be given, and he will have abundance; but from him who does not have, even what he has will be taken away. And cast the unprofitable servant into the outer darkness. There will be weeping and gnashing of teeth" (Matthew 25:25, 28-30).

The key to understanding the parable is in what Jesus meant by the talent. What is the one thing He promised to entrust to us? The abundant life. And He wants to know what we have done with it. For our teaching about joy, the point is very clear. Those who multiply the gift of new life in Him enter into His joy. There is one kind of joy we receive in companionship with the Lord in prayer. There is an even greater joy which comes to us in adventuring with Him in involvement with people. To "enter into the joy of the Master" (with a capital M), is to share with others what He means to us. Whatever word you attach to it—soul-winning, sharing the faith, evangelism—matters little if the passion of our lives is bringing people to the Lord. We cannot experience deeper joy, or keep it, until we share the love we have received.

Some of us are too busy for that. We refuse to be interrupted by people who are put on our agendas by the Lord. Many of us do not want a life where plans are apt to be canceled for situations of unscheduled human need. There is little place or time for sudden, unrepeatable opportunities to incarnate an act of divine love. We get hung up on what we perceive as our own spiritual maturity, a petulant perfectionism over theological details, or do's and don'ts which have little to do with Christ's purpose for us. Many have never discovered that an act of extending love or telling another what Christ can do with a life surrendered to Him explodes into joy!

Needy candidates for Christ's love are all around us. Love-starved people are everywhere. Unblessed children of loveless marriages. Distraught parents. People locked into the syndrome of sameness. Friends who are anxious and worried. Associates who are missing the reason they were born. Neighbors tied like Gulliver to the accumulation of things, and acquaintances who are more ready to talk about their heartaches than we are to listen. Some of those people will not know joy now and may not live forever because we hid the talent of our abundant life in the ground.

Have I written myself into a contradiction? How can the fruit of the Spirit of joy be freely given and yet depend so much on our response? All I have tried to say is that which we will not use, we lose. Joy is ours as a result of grace. But it is for the realities of life. And it lasts as long as it is given away.

Robert Louis Stevenson was right: "To miss the joy is to miss all."

Peace Be *IN* You

What robs you of peace? What makes you impatient and stretches you to the breaking point? These are precisely the points at which the Spirit can give you peace.

Peace Be *IN* You

I AM GOING TO ASK YOU some very personal questions. Audacious? Maybe. But if you and I could sit down and talk together over a cup of coffee, these are the questions I would like to ask you—and I would like you to ask me:

What is it that robs you of peace?

Who is it in your life who hassles you to the point where you lose your inner calm—that sense of unity and peace?

What is it in your life that makes you impatient and stretches your innermost self to the place of breaking?

Who is it who can rankle you to the place that you lose your countenance and blast that person for what he or she is or has done?

We all have a breaking point, a place where life gets to us, when it is impossible to feel peace or express patience. Here the fallacy hits us once again. We have been taught all our lives that peace was something we could condition by thinking the right thoughts.

There is nothing wrong with good mental hygiene, but the peace that will see us through the deep turbulence of our times is not programmed mind-control. Such peace cannot be induced by drugs or patched into the fabric of our tissues like an electrode.

Peace is the pearl we would give fortunes for. "Peace," Matthew Henry said, "is such a precious jewel that I would give anything for it but truth."

The fruit of the Spirit is peace.

LONGING FOR PEACE

Our mental institutions are filled with people longing for peace. Walk along any street in any city in America. We can all see the expressions on the faces of people that indicate a lack of peace in their hearts.

Is it any wonder the word was so often on the lips of our Lord? He greeted His disciples with the single word, "Peace!" The early church was characterized by the greeting, "The peace of the Lord Jesus be with you!" A part of the historic eucharist has been: *"Pax tibiti"*—"Peace to you!"

In Hebrew the word for "peace" is *shalom.* In Greek it is *eirene.* In Latin it is *pax.* What is this peace?

Peace is more than a state of freedom from hostility, more than harmony or a temporary truce in personal relationships. We need to plumb deeply into the nature of the peace our Lord had in mind when He said: "Peace I leave with you, my peace I give to you; not as the world gives do I give to you. Let not your heart be troubled, neither let it be afraid" (John 14:27).

He gives it to us by virtue of His indwelling presence, the presence Paul spoke of as fruit to imply a process of growth, or degrees of development depending on our cooperation. The fruit of peace becomes resplendent in us when our acceptance of God's forgiveness is complete in every level of our being.

There are memories that lurk within us and rob us of peace, memories that rub the conscience raw. When we are quiet, a familiar piece of music, or a face we have not seen for a long time, floods back into our minds and hearts, bringing with it the realization of unresolved failure, sin, or rebellion. And our peace is gone.

Our peace is also shattered when we refuse to be the agent of forgiveness in the lives of other people. Is there anyone you need to forgive, anyone who has failed you at some point in your life—in your family, the church, or in our society? Very often we carry the burden of the hurt and resentment and actually live as though Christ had not made a once, never-to-be-repeated, substitutionary reconciliation for the sin of the world in His body on the Cross. "For it pleased the Father that in Him all the fullness should dwell, and by Him to reconcile all things to Himself, by Him, whether things on earth or things in heaven, having made peace through the blood of His Cross" (Colossians 1:19-20).

We either accept or try to reproduce that magnificent atonement. And very often we fail to forgive all. We take the burden of some failure in another person's life and carry it inside ourselves. We do it at the cost of trying to reproduce what was done at Calvary on our behalf. "A great many people are trying to make peace," D.L. Moody said, "but that has already been done. God has not left it for us to do; all we have to do is to enter into it."

Second place is the only place Christ will not take. He was rather severe about the nature of the peace He would offer when He said, "Do not think that I came to bring peace on earth; I have not come to bring peace but a sword" (Matthew 10:34). Suddenly our minds are awake to discover the kind of severing He meant. "He who loves father or mother more than Me is not worthy of Me; and he who loves son or daughter more than Me is not worthy of Me.... He who finds His life will lose it, and He who loses His life for My sake will find it" (Matthew 10:37, 39).

A lack of peace is a warning signal, a jarring alarm inside us telling us that someone or something has taken Christ's place as Lord of our hearts. Who is it? What is it? Where is it for you?

We all long to be quiet inside, to have an inner unity and oneness. The loss of this peace is the price we pay for a secondary loyalty. Jesus Christ said we cannot possibly serve two masters. Authentic love of one results in hatred for the other. Anytime you feel terrible dis-ease and dis-quiet it is time to begin to ask, "Who's first in my life? Am I seeking first God's kingdom, His absolute reign and rule in all of life's relationships and responsibilities?"

DO YOU HAVE PEACE?

Are you at peace right now? Is there within you that quiet, healing distillation, that only the Lord can give?

The meaning of the word *peace* in Greek is the knitting-together, the unification of what has been broken and unraveled and disrupted. It means wholeness. In fact, in Hebrew, it's almost a synonym for the meaning of *salvation,* which means deliverance, oneness, wholeness and unification.

Do I have peace? It is only fair that you should ask me that question, too. I find that though I spend my life studying the Scriptures, leading a church, caring for people, and getting more than my share of love and affirmation from these relationships, there are times when I feel an absence of peace. Sometimes—for a moment, day, or a week—I take my eyes off Jesus Christ and put them on some cause or some purpose or something that I willfully want to do. That's when I begin to feel what I have come to call "jangledness" inside; I have to be still and go back to prayer and say, "Lord, what is it that has taken priority over You?"

Do you remember that marvelously clean and uncluttered sentence written by the prophet Isaiah on this very subject? "You will keep him in perfect peace, whose mind is stayed on You" (Isaiah 26:3). That is the answer.

Peace is the companion of knowing and doing the will of God. We cannot be at peace if we have been given marching orders in a particular relationship or sector of our lives and refuse to follow them. Once we say, "Lord, what do *You* want me to do? What do *You* want me to say? How do *You* want me to act?" and consciously refuse to follow the clear directive He gives, we will not know peace. Faithful obedience—that is the environment that develops the fruit of peace.

Paul used an athletic term to help the Colossian

Christians understand how the peace factor enables us to know what is creative for us, and what could be debilitating. He advised, "Let the peace of Christ rule in your hearts" (3:15). The Greek word for "rule" means *umpire*. The indwelling Christ will call the plays—safe or out.

The apostle also spoke of peace as a protector. Listen to this: "Be anxious for nothing, but in everything, by prayer and supplication, with thanksgiving, let your requests be made known to God; and the peace of God, which surpasses all understanding will guard your hearts and minds through Christ Jesus" (Philippians 4:6-7).

The word for "guard" in the phrase "guard your hearts and minds" means to garrison, to watch out for, to stand as a sentinel. Paul uses a military word in Greek, *phrourein,* "standing on guard." Christ's spirit is within us on round-the-clock duty, guarding, watching for approaching danger, sounding the warning-signal, defending us from all that would produce panic in our hearts. When we trust Him, there is peace.

MAKING PEACE WITH OTHERS

It is one thing to have peace, to savor peace, to be managed and protected by this divine implant of the Spirit. But there is one thing more: You can be the Lord's agent in making peace for others. "Blessed are the peacemakers," Jesus said, "for they shall be called sons of God" (Matthew 5:9). The dividends from such an investment of yourself have no equal. To be a peacemaker means to be actively involved with God in the task of reconciling people to Himself.

The fruit of peace bears fruit. The fruit of one Christian is another. We are to be reproductive. Our Christian life is not complete until we become active, contagious communicators of Christ's love to others. Each of us was introduced to the Savior by someone who cared enough to become involved in listening and loving. I would not be writing this book if it had not been that two college friends took time to earn the right to show me that my emptiness was a longing for purpose and power which only Christ could give. I saw the peace of Christ in them and wanted what they had. Who is alive in Christ because of you? Who in your life most needs an introduction to Peace Himself? Your concern for them is a call to tell them what He has done for you and then, when he or she has been prepared by the Spirit, to be the winsome introducer.

We cannot make peace by ourselves. It is Spirit-grown. But each of us can be God's agent in "making" peace with others. That means taking initiative: being the first to ask for or express forgiveness and restitution.

Each of us can also be God's special agent in reconciling people to each other, as an unassuming, "unofficial" peace presence in the tensions that explode around us. We are to listen to both sides without taking sides. We can go to people who are separated in conflict and misunderstanding. Our task is to open the channels of understanding and empathy. Often it is necessary to help people pray for forgiveness and the power to be forgiving.

We will feel the pulse of the heart of God as when He yearned over Israel. "They have healed the wound of my people lightly, saying, 'Peace, peace,' when there is no peace" (Jeremiah 8:11, RSV). Whenever we get in touch with the anguish in people or whenever we identify our own struggles, we realize how much we need the peace of God and how much we need to become peacemakers. The Spirit's peace in us can add a sacramental touch to shared joys and sorrows.

Peace flows into us when we allow it to flow out of us in active peacemaking. A child shares the character and purpose of his or her father. We are truly sons and daughters of God when we are engaged in active peacemaking. Today is the time for initiating peace. Anything which keeps people apart is our concern and responsibility as peacemakers. If we want Christ's peace in our hearts, we must be engaged in combating negative criticism, gossip, and innuendos which destroy relationships. Our constant concern will be to help people forgive, accept, and understand one another. Think of what life could be if our purpose were to bring reconciliation among our families and friends! Here is a daily motto. Put it on your desk, on the wall of your kitchen, or beside your bed to read when you start each day. "God was in Christ reconciling the world to Himself, not counting their trespasses against them, and entrusting to us the message of reconciliation. So we are ambassadors for Christ, God making His appeal through us" (2 Corinthians 5:19-20, RSV).

Finally, peace is the result of the indwelling of the living Christ. Peace is not only a gift of Christ, it is Christ Himself living His life in us through the Holy Spirit, His presence in our hearts and minds. It is abiding in Christ and allowing Him to abide in us.

Our Lord gives us the gift to be able to picture what

we would be like if His peace dwelt in our hearts. Imagine yourself as a peace-possessed person. Now picture the peace of Christ's love and forgiveness flowing among all your loved ones and friends.

Prayer for peace comes from a lively, Christ-inspired imagination. Once we have the picture, we can ask Christ to give us His legacy of peace. He is more ready to give than we are to ask. Praying for peace begins with Him. He motivates us to ask for what He has prepared for us through a manger, a Cross, an empty tomb, and a present power. Now we can say and mean, "Peace be with you! May the peace of the living Christ live in your hearts." The fruit of the Spirit is peace.

FIVE

Living on the Lord's Timing

Some of us have an "inner horn" that we blow when life's traffic seems too heavy and things don't go our way. How can we learn patience in an impatient world?

Living on
the Lord's Timing

T HE SHORTEST MOMENT in time occurs when you are
stopped in your car at an intersection. It's the split
second between the instant that the traffic light turns
green and when the person in the car or truck behind
you leans on his horn impatiently.

This time it was no ordinary horn. The blaring blast
almost lifted me off my seat. Startled, I checked my rear
view mirror. A gigantic Mack truck with an ominous
looking grill was behind me. A grim-faced driver was
shaking his fist. I checked the traffic light. It was just now
turning green! Another fierce blast of the horn—I got
moving as quickly as I could.

Not fast enough, though, for the truck driver behind
me; no matter how fast I drove, I couldn't get away from
him. At any moment I thought he was going to drive
that motorized projection of his ego right up over the
trunk of my car. Persistently he blew his imperious-
sounding horn.

Finally, after being tracked down for four blocks, I

pulled over to the curb and stopped my car. The truck sped past me with the driver again shaking his fist and shouting what I imagined were obscenities. Then, to my surprise, the truck swerved to the curb and parked in front of a store just ahead of where I had sought refuge.

I expected the driver to jump out of the cab of his truck and give me the unwelcome gift of a further piece of his impatient mind. Instead, he just sat there, aimlessly, as if he had nothing else to do. Apparently, his impatience had nothing to do with his delivery schedule.

I sat in my car for a moment before I drove on. I began to laugh at myself. I had been very impatient with people and situations that day. The Lord had allowed me to receive a strong dose of my own mood from this reckless, impatient truck driver.

Still chuckling to myself about the way the Lord uses situations to expose us to our impatient selves, I slowly drove my car up to the side of the truck. I rolled down the window on the passenger side and, with a thumbs-up signal, called out to the driver, "Hey, thanks for the message!"

As I drove on I thought of a wonderful retort given by a man whose car had stalled at an intersection. While the lights changed several times, a woman in the car behind him relentlessly blew her horn.

Finally, the man got out of his car and casually walked back to the woman. "Would you do me a favor?" he asked. "Please go up and try to get my car started while I sit in your car and blow the horn!"

That's the kind of clever remark we think about making hours after we've become impatient with someone's impatience!

TRYING TO BE PATIENT
IN AN IMPATIENT SOCIETY

But our impatience is not limited to blowing the horns of our cars. Many of us have an inner horn we blow when things don't go our way or people get in our way. Some of us are racehorses who get perturbed by the turtles who clutter up the racetrack of life.

We live in an impatient society catered to by fast-food restaurants, products which provide instant satisfaction, and a host of businesses which offer immediate service. An experience the other day brought this into sharp focus.

I was out of town, and I needed a suit cleaned and pressed in a hurry. I found one of those, "fresh as a flower in just one hour," quick cleaning establishments. The sign on the door said, "We cater to impatient people in a hurry." Feeling that I qualified on both counts, I presented my crumpled, well-traveled suit to the owner. He took my name and with an unpleasant attitude demanded, "When do you want it? Yesterday, I suppose!"

My first inclination was to grab my suit back and tell him that he could keep his cleaning fluids and the juices of his unpleasantness to himself, but my pride got the best of me when I thought of speaking in that wrinkled suit. I pointed to the sign with all the one-hour, for-people-in-a-hurry promises. "Yeah, that's right," he said tempering his tone a bit. "It's been a hard day. I guess I'm impatient with impatient people!" We both laughed, the tension was relaxed, and he cleaned and pressed my suit... in a hurry!

As I walked back to my hotel, I reflected on the living

parable I had just experienced. The very thing that shop wanted to be known for was the one thing the proprietor was tired of producing. He wanted to serve impatient people and yet his impatience bristled when asked to do what the sign promised.

Then it hit me: I would like to be known as a patient person. I preach about it, try to help others discover it, and yet I find impatience a difficult problem to conquer. I had never met the cleaning man before, and yet his diagnosis was on target: I do like to have everything yesterday!

How about you? Ever troubled with impatience? Do difficult people test your patience? Does what they do or fail to do get to you? Are you ever upset when people you love fail to capture the vision you have for them? Ever get exasperated when people do not meet your expectations of what you want them to accomplish on your time schedule? And more profoundly, knowing people's potential and what the Lord can do with a life given over to His control, do you become impatient with their slow response or imperviousness?

And what about the problems in our society and the world? Does reading the newspaper fill you with indignation? With all our scientific advancement and technological skill, we have not come very far in human progress. Or, what about the slowness of governmental machinery? Does your blood boil over our ineptness and inefficiency in grasping and solving problems? To top it off, there is the computerized impersonalization of modern business. Have you tried to straighten out a bill you have overpaid or underpaid? And behind it all are people whose goofs and oversights gum up the highly polished machinery. People like you and me!

Another source of our impatience is ourselves. Have you been astounded, as I have at myself, by the little progress you've made in some areas? In your personal life and attitudes? Your relationships? Your work and professional advancement? Most of us could qualify for the sign in the quick-cleaning shop. We are impatient and in a hurry. But where are we going so fast?

If we were to get where we are going, where would we be? If we acquired all that we want, what would we have? When it is all over, what is the one-word epitaph they could put on our gravestone? Patient? Not I, nor most of us.

But let's not be too severe with ourselves. Go deeper. Our real problem is finding the balance between a divinely inspired discontent and simply accepting ourselves and things as they are. We are thankful for the reformers, inventors, and visionaries of history who did not accept the lie that what is must always be. The people who helped history turn its crucial corners were people who had a dream and dared to stick with it. They were patient and *creatively impatient* all at the same time. Endurance marked their characters. They persisted with the vision until it came of age.

Perhaps our problem with *im*patience is that we misunderstand *patience*. It is not acquiescence, or perpetual placidity, or feckless lack of fiber. Patience must be rooted in an over-arching confidence that there is Someone in control of this universe, our world, and our lives. We need to know that God works things together for good for those who love Him (Romans 8:28). A patient person knows the shortness of time and the length of eternity. *Patience is faith in action.*

IMPATIENT WITH GOD

Now we have come to the real source of our impatience: we are really impatient with God! Sometimes we call it the problem of unanswered prayer. Most often, it's simply that we can't get God marching to the cadence of what we want when we want it. The most frustrating word in our lexicon is "wait." We run ahead of God in what we desire and lag behind in doing what He desires of us.

Impatience becomes a flaw in our character when we pull away from walking with God. The prophet Amos asked, "Can two walk together unless they are agreed?" (Amos 3:3). The Hebrew word translated as "agreed" can also mean "met." Can two walk together unless they have met? Of course not. There must be a meeting place from which they begin to walk together. Then they must walk at the same pace toward a shared destination. Calvary is the place where we meet God in His ultimate revelation of His patient, long-suffering grace and mercy.

Patience is really an attribute of God. When He met Moses on Mount Sinai, God's own self-disclosure was, "The Lord, the Lord God, merciful and gracious, *long-suffering*, and abounding in goodness and truth" (Exodus 34:6). Moses used these very words when he later prayed for God's patience with Israel. The psalmist claimed God's patience when he pulled out all the stops in soaring adoration, "Bless the Lord O my soul and all that is within me bless His holy name.... The Lord is merciful and gracious, slow to anger and abounding in mercy" (Psalm 103:1,8). Here the Hebrew words for "slow to anger" literally mean, "long in the nostrils!" The idea was that anger was vented from the nostrils and God's patience with His people was long and enduring. The prophet Joel knew this and called Judah to "return to the Lord your God, for He is gracious and merciful, slow to anger, and of great kindness" (Joel 2:13).

We discover what patience *is* from God. He has all the time in the world. And He is on time with His interventions to help us, in time with His guidance and forgiveness. Micah declared the secret of learning to live patiently. It's a part of our walk. We are "to walk humbly with God" (Micah 6:8). Here the Hebrew word translated as "humbly" means "attentively." Walking attentively is to listen to what God has to say to us about His patience and the patience He wants us to experience.

God's word to us about patience has been spoken in the Word, Christ Jesus. In Christ we see patience incarnate. It was a vital trait in the character He came to reveal. Living on God's timing, Christ was never in a hurry. Saturated with prayer, He sought only to know and do His Father's will. Christ's obedience led to the Cross and His atoning death for our forgiveness. All so that when He rose victoriously from the grave, He could call into being a new creation of creatures in whom He could engender His own character.

True patience is a supernatural character trait. It is a part of the fruit of the Spirit given to those who believe in Christ as Savior and Lord *and* are filled with His Spirit. Patience is the mysterious fruition of love, joy, and peace.

The fruit of the Spirit is patience.

ONLY ONE PERSON
CAN TEACH US TO BE PATIENT

If we would learn patience, Christ alone can teach us. There are many facsimiles of this character trait, but authentic, lasting patience comes as a result of a deep personal relationship with Christ.

The original Greek word Paul used for patience in the list of the fruit of the Spirit is *makrothumia.* It's a compound word: *makros*—"long or far," and *thumos*—"hot, anger, wrath or temper." Patience is long or slow anger, or long-tempered. "Temper" is a word that describes the quality of our attitudes, the characteristic frame of our minds. Another way of putting it is that attitudes are congealed thought and the expression of those attitudes comprises our temperament. We talk about quick-tempered or even-tempered people. The fruit of Christ's Spirit in us makes us *long*-tempered.

Another word for patience in the New Testament is *hupomone.* It reveals how we become long-tempered. *Hupomone* also is a compound word: *hupo*—"under," *meno*—"to abide." When the Spirit of Christ abides in us, we abide under His control. We are enabled by Him to wait for His perspective and power. If we trust Him, He will guide us in how we are to react and what we are to say. Our temperament is transformed by Christ in us. Mysteriously, the transplant of His character trait of patience is planted in us and begins to grow. He reminds us of His unqualified love and forgiveness, His indefatigable patience with us in our failures, and His repeated interventions to help us. Christ never gives up on us. And as we abide under His gracious care, we discover a new power to be long-tempered, that is, patient, with ourselves and others. But the wonder of it all is that He is the patience we are able to express.

The process of becoming a patient person happens in the school of Christ. It takes place when we are yoked with Him. He has given us the secret of the fruit of His indwelling presence. "Come to me, all who labor and are heavy laden, and I will give you rest. Take My yoke upon you, and learn from Me; for I am gentle and lowly in heart, and you will find rest for your souls. For my yoke is easy, and my burden is light" (Matthew 11:28-30).

The Lord's invitation and promise gives us four salient aspects of how to learn to be patient in His style and by His power.

IF THE YOKE FITS, WEAR IT!

First of all, Jesus knows about our frustrations and the resulting anger over things, people, and ourselves. To labor and still be heavy laden is to feel trapped by life and by its constricting circumstances. The Lord felt deeply the pain of the economic, political, and religious yokes under which people lived. The future offered little relief. Most of the people were poor. The heel of Rome pressed tightly on their necks with taxes and restrictions of a captured people in an occupied land. But of greatest concern to the Master was the people's endless labor to do the works of the law with faithfulness and their attempt to carry burdens placed upon them by the scribes with their endless rules and regulations. Christ appealed to people who had tried to please God by fulfilling the letter of the law and failed. His invitation has echoed down through the centuries to people who are burdened by life and their own inability to change themselves or the life around them.

Jesus Christ invites the impatient to come to Him, those who have tried to be faithful and creative and have not been able to pull it off. Only a person who has values, standards, and a vision of what life can be is impatient with himself, other people, or circumstances. In substance, He says to us, "Come to me, I understand the disappointment and frustration you feel. I know your integrity and the heartache you experience when you miss the mark. I want to give you a gift—an entirely new way to live."

The second dynamic of this verse tells how Christ proposes to impart this precious gift. He offers an exchange of yokes. To people under a yoke He offers a new yoke. Instead of the yoke of heavy burdens, He offers His own yoke of freedom. We need to think about that.

Two tributaries of ancient parlance and practice flow together to form a vivid image of what the yoke means. The rabbis of the time spoke of the yoke relationship of a student with his teacher. The word *yoke* was a synonym for school. This is surely part of what Jesus meant, for He followed His challenge to take His yoke with the invitation to learn of Him.

Further, investigation into the eastern methods of plowing helps us to understand what Jesus meant by the yoke. Mosaic law forbade an old and a young ox to be hitched together in an ordinary yoke. This was because the young animal could not pull his part of the burden. The phrase "unequally yoked" comes from this. A training yoke was required by law. The heavy end of the yoke was the burden of the stronger, older beast. The experienced bovine kept the furrow straight and, under the reigns of the plowman, moved forward. All the younger beast had to do was to keep parallel with the stronger animal; if it pulled away, ahead or behind, its neck would be rubbed raw in the yoke. The trainee had to give up the right to lead in order to keep pace with the trainer. The lead ox must take the lead and the responsibility for the burden. Now it begins to dawn on us what Christ meant when He offered us His yoke as a source of freedom... and patience.

Our minds leap to the implication. Christ carries the heavy end of the yoke. He pulls the burden for us. We must give up our wills to Him. Patience is developed in the school of Christ. We are yoked with Him to discover how to live with His guidance, strategy, and timing. Impatience involves running ahead, pulling off in our own direction, or stomping our feet in petulant pouting. Patience is developed through keeping a parallel pace with the Master. The cadence of His perfect will in our lives sets the rhythm for a life of peace.

We all know what it is like to be rubbed raw by our own impatience. We have all tried to accomplish our goals with only our own strength; and equally defeating, we have tried to do His work on our strength. It will not work. We become impatient when we want to do what we want, when we want it, and with whom we want it. Who has not bashed down a closed door while an open door stood nearby, with the Master inviting us to follow Him inside?

To be in a training yoke with Christ means several

magnificent gifts are offered to us. He carries the burden! We were never created to live the Christian life on
our own. The source of our strength is in surrendering
our burdens to Him. As soon as we are yoked with
Christ, the load is lifted. All we have to do is keep pace.
Bernard of Clairvaux explained that such a yoke is a
blessed burden that makes all burdens light, a yoke that
bears the bearer up.

In the yoke with Christ, we can give up the responsibility of running the universe. We can have intimate
communion with the Lord at all times. Our times are in
His hands. He knows what He is doing.

When was the last time you told Him you knew that
and completely turned over to Him the direction,
desires, and duration of your life's furrow? Patience is
the fruit of that yoke union.

Thomas à Kempis said that if we wanted to be free to
persist in our own will, then we would never be peaceful
or free from care. Impatience really is breaking the first
commandment. It is making ourselves a god over our
own lives. It does not work. It has not since the beginning of time.

Being a yokefellow with Christ assures us of guidance
and direction. If we ask Him, and abide in Him until the
answer becomes clear, we will feel release from tension.
We will not panic. The Lord who gives each day will
show the way.

That is what He means when He says, "My yoke is easy
and my burden light." The word for "easy" is *chrestos* in
the Greek text. It means kindly, a divine offer. At that
time, the word *kindness* was used only for God. Jesus as

the Messiah, the I Am, was the only one who could make such an offer.

As we'll discover in the next chapter, kindness implies empathy, understanding, forgiveness, and a constant flow of second chances. God is sublimely kind to us, and that kindness was manifested in His Son's life and sacrificial death. Jesus is telling us that to be yoked with Him is to experience a continuous flow of kindness. Such a yoking enables true patience, first with ourselves, then with our shortcomings, and then with others and their failures and inability to meet our standards.

But also note the further assurance of the way that Jesus helps us when we are yoked to Him. His burden is light. That can mean either that we have the light end of the training yoke, or that, as He carries the heavier end of the training yoke, He is yoked with God Himself. During His ministry, Jesus exemplified the quality of dependent trust in God which He wanted His followers to emulate. His constant and consistent communion with God in times of prayer and repeated relinquishment of His own will give the secret of the right balance between divinely inspired discontent with where we are at and trust in the Lord's final justice and grace.

The third aspect of this verse is focused on what Jesus teaches us while we are yoked to Him. He tells us that He is "gentle and lowly in heart." The King James version of the Bible renders it "meek and lowly." The words mean leadable, open to be guided, teachable, receptive. One of the uses of the word *meek* was for an animal which had been broken and would follow the lead of the reins. An impatient person is the opposite of this. Impatience is bucking, refusing to be guided, and taking things into our own control. It is demanding that things go our way, on our schedule, regardless of cost. (We'll have more to say about that when we consider the fruit of gentleness.)

The fourth aspect of Christ's salient secret for the cure of impatience is that the yoke of Christ provides rest for our souls. The Lord promised that if we become yokefellows with Him we would need consistent times of rest. As the leader of our yoked-training with Him, He will not only lead the way and determine the pace, but He will also know when to stop us in our tracks. The word *rest* in this verse means refreshment. The Lord refreshes us by renewing our inner conviction that He is the source of our wisdom and guidance, and of strategic timing. It is when we are quiet that we know that He is able to do all things well and is worthy of our trust.

Years ago, philosopher William Ernest Hocking in his classic, *The Meaning of God in Human Experience,* elucidated what he called the "principles of alternation." We need times of rest to regain our perspective and power. When we go without deliberate pauses, we begin to get in our own way, and thus we defeat our own work.

I know this is true from my own experience. I am most impatient when I am overtired, spiritually exhausted, or emotionally drained. Since the major cause of impatience with others and circumstances is impatience with ourselves, we need times when we allow the Lord to heal our depleted self-esteem and renew our delight in being the unique miracle He created us to be.

A busy physician once told me that he was going off for a week of silence on a retreat. "I need to fall in love again—with the Lord, myself, people, and life, in that order!" Not a bad prescription for healing impatience. In the clamorous din around us and in us, we need to listen again to the voice of the Lord's gentle stillness.

Leonardo da Vinci was asked why he had long periods of inactivity while he was painting *The Last Supper.* He said that when he paused the longest, it was then that he made the most telling strokes with his brush. The same is true for us. We require quiet intervals if we are to win the battle with impatience. It may seem strange to you that quiet, prayerful inactivity and meditation would help impatience. Why not get on with it, get at the task and finish it? The problem is that tension mounts, and we become ineffective.

The Lord told the psalmist, "Be still and know that I am God." When the psalmist followed the Lord's directive, he was able finally to write the admonition, "Wait on the Lord; be of good courage, and He shall strengthen your heart; wait, I say, on the Lord!" (Psalm 27:14). "My soul, wait silently for God alone, for my expectation is from Him" (Psalm 62:5). Note the progression: wait, receive courage, and go forward with strength. Without resting in the Lord, our impatience causes impetuousness. Our greatest errors and strained relationships come when we have lost touch with the Lord's inner guidance and wisdom.

Frederick W. Faber expressed how we must wait for God. We must wait long, meekly, in wind and wet, in the thunder and lightning, in the cold and the dark. We must wait, and He will come. But God never comes to those who do not wait.

It is in the waiting times that our most creative

thoughts and plans are formulated. Instead of rushing headlong in our own impatience, the Lord is able to tell us what are the next steps and how we are to move forward in His strategy for us and the people around us.

When Dante appeared at the Franciscan monastery door, a monk opened the door and asked him what he wanted. "Peace!" was Dante's one word answer. That eventually became the Lord's gift to him when he learned to wait, pray, and listen. Later, in *The Divine Comedy*, he wrote his oft-quoted line, "In His will is our peace." The refreshment of Christ is peace to replace our impatience. Then we can pray with Richard of Chichester, the thirteenth-century saint,

> O most merciful Redeemer, Friend
> and Brother, may we know Thee
> more clearly, love Thee more dearly,
> and follow Thee more nearly; for
> Thine own sake. —Amen.

Christ is peace. Christ is patience. We could never produce these graces on our own strength, in the quantities that are needed in our families and our world. But we do have access to an unlimited stockpile of patience, when the fruit of the Spirit of patience gives us courage to live on His timing and act with His power.

When You're Down on Yourself

Even "up" people sometimes get down on themselves. We are haunted by our failures, by our inability to be the people we would like to be. Only God's kindness, only His steadfast love, heals our sense of unworthiness.

When You're Down
on Yourself

D O YOU EVER GET down on yourself? It happens to all of us at times, whenever we feel we do not measure up to our own standards. It attacks when we fail to do what we planned, or compulsively repeat old habits we thought we had left behind. Our accomplishments do not match our expectations. Dreams are unfulfilled, hopes are dashed, and agendas are tardy. Who's to blame? "I am!" we say to ourselves. The "if onlys" of the past invade the "what ifs" of the present. We are engulfed in a sense of guilt. "If I had been different... if I had worked harder... if I had been wiser... if I had been stronger," becomes the dirge of self-incrimination.

We all have an awesome capacity for self-scrutiny. We can analyze our own performances and personalities. Coupled with that is our capacity to remember; we are haunted by old memories of what we did that we shouldn't have done, and what we should have done that we never accomplished. That's when we become our own parents, or our own diminutive god, and take over the punishment of ourselves. Discouragement and depression result. Our conscience shakes an accusing finger.

Self-condemnation sets in. Self-esteem drains out. We begin to feel bad about ourselves. Self-negation dominates our feelings. It is then that we are the most vulnerable, and the most apt to do what we promised ourselves we would never do: we act out our depleted self-image. Others are treated the way we treat ourselves. We become unkind in word and action. Our sense of guilt thrashes about searching for something to do which will support negative self-appraisal—all so we can say to ourselves, "See, what you did is what you are!"

It is difficult to get up for life when we are down on ourselves. What can we do about our sense of guilt, self-negation, and resultant self-condemnation? What would it take to give us a whole new picture of ourselves as loved and lovable, forgiven and forgiving?

A POOR "FORGETTER"

I talked to a man who was down on himself. After he had told me all the things he could muster to support his bad feelings about himself, he said a stunning thing, "If I could only forget the failures and remember the accomplishments, I'd be okay—I've got a good memory and a poor forgetter."

A poor forgetter! The word is not in the dictionary. It should be. Allow me to venture a definition: A "forgetter" is the capacity to forget the failures and inadequacies of the past. What we remember and what we forget is crucial for our spiritual and mental health. The only way to get up when we are down on ourselves is to have our memories healed and our forgetters strengthened.

The great French philosopher Henri Bergson said that it is the function of the brain to not only remember but to also forget. We laugh, "I must have a super brain because of all the things I forget!" Who has not forgotten someone's birthday or an important date on our calendars. We do not need training in forgetfulness. We are highly trained experts in that! But why is it that we forget things we want to remember and remember things we long to forget? Why is it that one failure sticks in our memory and hundreds of achievements are forgotten? There are lots of self-improvement courses available for memory training, but I have never seen one on how to forget. Yet our inability to forget gives our compulsive conscience lots of accusing ammunition. We need just as much help in developing our "forgetter."

We cannot do that for ourselves. We are immobilized by feelings of guilt. Others cannot help us. They are either too down on themselves to help, or too glib in their encouraging affirmations to be taken seriously. It does not help for someone to tell us we are great if we feel gross. Their accolades are dismissed by our incriminating self. "If they only knew! They wouldn't be so magnanimous."

LEARNING SELF-FORGIVENESS

A healthy forgetter is developed by forgiveness. We cannot erase the memory cards of our failures in our brain computers until we have a profound experience of forgiveness. The authentic mark of truly mature persons is the capacity to forgive themselves. What a rare commodity! Years of experience in seeking to be a whole person, and helping others with their self-esteem, have led me to the conclusion that one of the greatest miracles of life is self-forgiveness. I have never known a person who has been able to do it without a healing experience of Christ's kindness.

The purpose of this chapter is to plumb the depths of self-condemnation and to show how Christ's kindness can help us get up when we are down on ourselves. His kindness *for* us enables a kindness *in* us for ourselves, and then for others.

The fruit of the Spirit is kindness.

THE SHEER KINDNESS OF GOD

Kindness is the steadfast love of the Lord in action toward those who fail and to those in need. Throughout the Old Testament, the words for steadfast love, mercy, kindness, and loving-kindness are used interchangeably to translate the Hebrew word *hesed*. It is the covenant word that expresses God's persistent, pursuing effort to reach His chosen, called, and cherished people and enable them to return to Him. *Hesed* is one of the three attributes of His nature that God especially wants His people to know and experience. "Let not the wise man glory in his wisdom, let not the mighty man glory in his might, let not the rich man glory in his riches; but let him who glories glory in this, that he understands and knows Me, that I AM the Lord exercising *loving-kindness*, judgment, and righteousness in the earth" (Jeremiah 9:23-24, italics added).

God's kindness is His prevenient, unmotivated love at the heart of His nature, offered not because we deserve it or even because we pray long and hard enough to think we have earned it. This kindness of God is not motivated into action because of how good or bad we are. He is kind to us not because of what we've said or done. God is kind because that is His nature, and in kindness, He constantly seeks to reach us in our lost and lonely estrangement from Him.

The Incarnation was the most convincing, undeniable evidence of God's kindness. God came in Christ out of sheer kindness. Jesus the Christ was kindness incarnate. He came to express it; lived to model it; died to offer it to us. He went to the Cross not because people asked for a sacrifice for their sins, but because, out of kindness, God willed to redeem us. God raised Christ from the dead as a final victory over the power of death and evil and made Him reigning Lord over the church with authority to baptize His followers with the Holy Spirit.

Peter expressed the wonder of this kindness in the first Christian sermon after Pentecost: "This Jesus God has raised up, of which we are all witnesses. Therefore being exalted to the right hand of God, and having received from the Father the promise of the Holy Spirit, He poured out this which you now see and hear" (Acts 2:32-33).

A new breed of humanity was created: women and men overwhelmed by the kindness of God in Christ. And through the indwelling of the Spirit of Christ in them, they discovered that they could now express to others the kindness they had received.

One who became the recipient of this amazing kindness of the early Christians was a Pharisee who was determined to persecute them. His name was Saul of Tarsus. Through the witness of the Christians in Damascus, the vigilant Pharisee experienced for himself the kindness of Christ. He became a new creature in Christ. His rigid hostility toward others and himself was melted by Christ's unsurpassed kindness. After fourteen years of secluded prayer and study, Paul was a new man ready to spread to the then-known world the good news of the kindness of God's love and forgiveness in Christ.

This triumphant grace note in the apostle's message is expressed in Ephesians 2:4-7, "But God, who is rich in mercy, because of His great love with which He loved us, even when we were dead in trespasses, made us alive together, and made us to sit together in the heavenly places in Christ Jesus, that in the ages to come He might show the exceeding riches of His grace in His *kindness* toward us in Christ Jesus" (italics added).

The Lord never demands anything from us that He is not willing to give us. It should not be surprising, then, that the power to be kind is available under the code name of fruit. Paul discovered that kindness is implanted, imputed, and ingrained into the very nature of our new heredity in Christ Jesus. It is a fruit of the Spirit in us, and, like love, joy, peace, and patience, it has a supernatural origin, a progressive growth and an undeniable fruition in our character. Kindness can now be expressed to ourselves and in our relationships with others.

The Greek word Paul used for kindness is *chrestotes*. When he speaks of the kindness of God it is used as an expression of His grace. "When the kindness and love of God our Savior toward men appeared, not by works of righteousness which we have done, but according to His mercy He saved us…" (Titus 3:4). As a part of Christ's character transplant, kindness enables us to be as merciful and gracious to ourselves and others as *Christ has been to us.*

One of the best ways to understand and appropriate Christ's kindness as a quality of our new character is to reflect on how He was kind to people during His ministry. When we live in the skin of those who received His kindness, expressed in gracious forgiveness, only then can we forgive ourselves "and be kind to one another, tenderhearted, forgiving one another, just as God in Christ also forgave you" (Ephesians 4:32).

KINDNESS TO AN UNFAITHFUL WOMAN

No encounter in Scripture reveals the kindness of Christ better than the account of the woman caught in adultery (John 7:53–8:11). What happened to the woman exemplifies what occurs when the kindness of Christ penetrates the dark places of hidden memories and remorse.

Put yourself in the scene: we are there in the crowd listening to the Master teach in the precincts of the Temple. Suddenly His teaching is interrupted by the jeers and frenzied cries of a crowd that approaches. A ghastly procession breaks through the crowd around

Jesus. It is led by scribes and Pharisees dragging an un-resisting woman. An angry, bloodthirsty mob follows close behind. They push her down before Jesus. She writhes in anguished sobs. What charge deserves this kind of treatment? It is obvious that she is no woman of the streets, no sensuous enticer of men's affections for a price. There is a dignity which has been crushed by this cruelty, a discernible longing which has been twisted and maligned.

Our hearts ache for the woman. We feel a combina-tion of embarrassment and shock. Our own hidden thoughts and memories are jabbed awake. Who has not had fantasies and feelings, if not actual failures, which, if exposed, would put us at Jesus' feet?

We look into the fiendishly frenzied faces of the scribes and Pharisees. Condemnation oozes from their every pore. Then our eyes fall on their hands. In each one is a large stone. They are ready to stone her! What crime deserves this? But we know the answer.

The scribes and Pharisees confirm our suspicions. "Teacher!" they say, addressing Jesus in supercilious mockery of His sacred title, "This woman was caught in adultery, in the very act." Their voices grow in self-righteous intensity. "Now Moses, in the law, commanded that such should be stoned. But what do You say?" Our minds leap back to the ancient Scriptures. We think of Leviticus 20:10, "The man who commits adultery with another man's wife, he who commits adultery with his neighbor's wife, the adulterer and the adulteress shall surely be put to death." The woman does not have a chance!

We look at her, crumpled and broken, before Jesus.

How do we feel about that charge? Questions begin to surge into our minds. Where is the man, if the woman was taken in the *very* act? Wasn't he equally guilty? And how did the scribes and Pharisees find her in her adulterous act? Could it have been staged? Is it possible that one of those holding a stone enticed her into the compromising indiscretion so the leaders could present Jesus with an impossible decision? But what was it that motivated the angry condemnation of these leaders?

Suddenly it dawns on us that they would have to have been down on themselves before they could make such a vitriolic attack on this woman. There is so much more than meets the eye here. These men are more hostile toward Jesus than they are toward the woman! Could it be that He has put a finger on a raw nerve in them through His teaching and preaching? Were they convicted before they convicted the woman?

Jesus is confronted with an impossible dilemma. If He denies the Law, He might be stoned Himself. If He sanctions the execution of the woman, He will be going against Rome, which has forbidden capital punishment by the Jews and their courts. There seems to be no way out. The condemning leaders have used a human being as a thing to trap Him. Jesus has gained the reputation of being a friend to sinners. Will this force Him to deny His compassionate ministry? We watch Him closely to observe what He will do.

We are deeply moved by the look on His face, as He stares into the faces of the angry mob and then down at the woman at His feet. She is too ashamed to lift her head.

Then, deliberately He stoops down. He lowers His

head. What is He doing? The silence is alarming. We all wait with bated breath.

With majestic authority He raises His hand, His forefinger extended with royal dignity. All eyes are immediately focused on that regal finger. Will He use it to point accusingly at the woman, at the leaders, or at us? Instead, He slowly, deliberately begins to write in the dusty sand of the ground. We strain our necks to see what He is writing. We cannot get close enough to discern it.

The leaders do not want to know. First one, and then another, begins to jibe and press Him in demanding tones. The crowd picks up the chant. "Give us an answer. The woman's guilty! Make your judgment!"

Jesus straightens to full height. Fire flashes from His eyes like lightning. The thunder of His voice follows quickly. It hits us like a blow. "He who is without sin among you, let him throw a stone at her first." A murmur of uneasiness grips the crowd. No one expected that. The tables have turned. Those who wanted to trap Jesus are now the ones who feel trapped.

Once again Jesus stops to write in the sand. What is He writing? It must be convicting, whatever it is, because now the leaders suddenly have panic on their faces. They look at each other with expressions that silently speak a frightened, "How did He know?" The Lord must be writing the commandments, or the hidden sins He discerned in these condemnatory leaders. Or could it be that He is writing the Hebrew word *hesed*, reminding the people of the mercy of God. Or is it the Hebrew letters for Yahweh, asserting that He, the Messiah, the I AM, has authority to judge and forgive?

Silence again. No one is moving a muscle. And then

the silence is broken by the thud of a large stone on the ground. We observe that the eldest of the Pharisees has dropped his stone. His judgment-worn face is twisted; now the hard lines of indignant superiority are softened a bit. Then there is another thud, and then another. The carefully selected, sharp, and craggy stones begin to rain down at the feet of the accusing, judgmental critics.

The woman cringes, expecting each one to hit her in judgment for her crime. She lifts her head in amazement as the leaders turn away, some in shame; others in grumbling defeat; others in retreat to find another chance to attack Jesus. From the eldest to the youngest, we want to leave, too. Nasty business this!

We feel anguish for the woman and anxiety for ourselves. We want to get out of there before Jesus writes our hidden sins upon the ground or reminds us of our merciless attitude toward ourselves, or toward someone like this woman.

We walk away hoping not to be noticed. Then, glancing back, we observe the most tender encounter we have ever seen. Jesus is still stooping, His finger in the sand. The broken woman looks up and her eyes meet His. Kindness radiates from His face. He stands up with measured movements, lifting the woman until they are face to face. We can hear what He says. Awesome Pity and a pitiful person meet. "Woman, where are those accusers of yours? Has no one condemned you?"

The woman looks around in amazement. "No one, Lord." It is as if Jesus wants to underline the fact that she is free of her accusers. But now, what about her own attitude toward herself? Will she be able to forget and make a new beginning?

Jesus' words of comfort and assurance are the most compassionate and authoritative ever spoken to anyone. We feel the impact of them as we listen. We are there in the woman's place. He takes us by the shoulders, looks deeply into our eyes and says, "Neither do I condemn you; go and sin no more."

Amazing! The sin is not condoned, but there is no condemnation. Kindness affording the power to forget.

Left to ponder what this means for us, we find ourselves in the skin of the accusers and the accused. Our unresolved guilt has caused us to act like those scribes and Pharisees more often than we want to remember. Our religion has prompted more condemnation than culpability. The more uneasy we are about our past, the more we get down on ourselves, and eventually, we become arrogant, religious prigs whose insecurity is expressed by being down on others.

But we are also forced to find ourselves at Jesus' feet, guilty as charged. No one has thrown us there. We have thrust ourselves there by our own self-condemnation. And the only hope of getting up from being down on ourselves is found in His words. Do you hear His kindness in your own soul? "Neither do I condemn you. Go and sin no more!"

Ever wonder what happened to the woman and her accusers after this confrontation of the destructive power of condemnation? Did the Pharisees and scribes become more kind? Perhaps some of them realized that their own feelings of guilt under the impact of Jesus' ministry had prompted them to be severe in their judgment of the woman. We would like to think that they began a new life of kindness toward others because of

Jesus' writing in the ground. But history testifies that, as a group, they never allowed the experience to affect their hearts or be expressed in their behavior. They continued with condemnation until they impaled Jesus, not only on the horns of a dilemma, but on a Cross. Religious judgmentalism dies hard, and is too seldom cured.

AN INSIDE LOOK

If we find ourselves among the accusers in this dramatic story, we have some painful questions to ask:

1. Do we ever escape our own self-condemnation by a critical, negative spirit to others?
2. Do we project onto others our own weary sense of guilt?
3. Do we expose and malign others for sins and failures we find in ourselves?
4. Do we hold others at a distance until they measure up?
5. Do we play God by meting out judgments and demanding that people atone to us for what they have done or been?
6. Have we been as merciful and gracious to others as our Lord has been to us?

But many of us find ourselves in the woman. Not only do we feel accused, but we accuse ourselves. Our failure may not be as obvious or easily categorized as the woman's, but what we are and have done is no less serious to our Lord.

To feel the full impact of the woman's plight and how Jesus dealt with her, we need to single out whatever it is that makes us feel down on ourselves right now. What is it for you? Whether it is great or small, it is the roadblock to healthy self-acceptance and self-esteem. Think about that as we grapple with how Jesus helps us to get up when we are down on ourselves.

Whatever the syndrome of loneliness or longing, the woman ended up more down on herself than the scribes and Pharisees could ever be. They only articulated what she already felt about herself. Their enacted exposure and judgment was nothing in comparison to what she had done to herself in her own mind a thousand times before. She had rendered the guilty charge on herself long before she was thrown at the feet of the Master.

The woman's own self-condemnation concerns the Lord most in this story. Once He got rid of the would-be accusers, He had to deal with the most vigilant accuser of all—the person inside the woman. Until she was as kind to herself as He was, she would not be free to live a new life. She had to change her mind about herself. Three things had to be accomplished. She needed radical forgiveness, remedial forgetfulness, and releasing freedom. And Jesus provided all three.

Radical forgiveness enables us to forgive ourselves. That can happen only if someone with an ultimate authority forgives us. Simply to forgive ourselves without the experience of forgiveness from another does not work. Jesus Christ has the authority and the power to forgive.

We have developed a lot of fancy words for our failures: maladjustment, neurosis, complexes, need-satisfaction, or emotional sickness. But only one word defines our condition—*sin*, separation from the Lord. Our deepest need is for reconciliation and relationship with Him. We are sinners. Our actions habitually break God's law for what He meant us to be. The Ten Commandments and Jesus' great commandment to love the Lord our God with all our mind, soul, and body have not gone out of style.

THE LAND OF BEGINNING AGAIN

Forgiveness gives us the hope of forgetting what is behind and moving on to live. We all long for that more than anything else. Louisa Fletcher Tarkington expresses how we all feel:

I wish that there were some wonderful place
   In the Land of Beginning Again:
Where all our mistakes and all our heartaches
   And all of our poor selfish grief
Could be dropped like a shabby old coat at the door
   And never put on again.

The land of beginning again is here and now. Jesus stands at the door welcoming us home from wherever we have wandered. This is the basis of remedial forgetfulness. We wonder what happened to the woman after she parted from the Master that day. Did she continue to condemn herself? Could she forget? Only if she could remember Jesus' words of kindness more than she remembered her sin. Robert Louis Stevenson said that it is our friends who stand between us and our self-contempt. And only Jesus can be that kind of friend who can close the door of the past and keep us from wandering furtively down the corridors of debilitating memory.

The central hope of the Christian faith is that we are new creatures in Christ—the old can pass away, the new can come! Listen to Paul who had a great deal to haunt him, "Forgetting those things which are behind and reaching forward to those things which are ahead, I press toward the goal for the prize of the upward call of God in Christ Jesus" (Philippians 3:13-14). That is why he could say, "Therefore, from now on, we regard no one according to the flesh [from a human point of view]. Even though we have known Christ according to the flesh, yet now we know Him thus no longer" (2 Corinthians 5:19).

What the apostle meant was that he no longer thought of Christ as one man among many. "God was in Christ reconciling the world to Himself" (2 Corinthians 5:19). On that basis, we no longer regard ourselves or others from the human perspective of judgment and condemnation. We are forgiven and released to forget. "Therefore, if any one is in Christ, he is a new creation; the old things have passed away, behold, all things have become new. Now all things are of God, who has reconciled us to Himself through Jesus Christ, not imputing their trespasses to them and has committed to us the word of reconciliation" (2 Corinthians 5:17-18). And that word of reconciliation begins with our own reconciliation to ourselves.

Only Christianity offers that. What a contrast with Mohammed, who said in the Koran that every man's fate is fastened about his neck and he is an accountant against himself. Not so with Christ. Christ has taken the sin and written "paid in full" across the ledger sheet of besetting memories.

The same capacity of the brain which we use to remember can be used *to remember to forget.* Each time the memory of our failure invades our consciousness and attacks our peace, we can recapture the experience of the kindness of our Lord and His forgiveness.

The only memories which have any power to stalk our present thoughts are those which have never been forgiven. If you have such memories, do battle with them right now. Look them in the face, and then tell the Lord about what you did or said. He lived and died for us, and He has forgiven us. We can sing with the psalmist, "For as the heavens are high above the earth, so great is His steadfast mercy toward those who fear Him; as far as the east is from the west, so far has He removed our transgressions from us" (Psalm 103:11-12).

Can we dare to say, "I can't forgive myself," if our Lord who created us and saved us has said, "I forgive you"? The ultimate blasphemy and the most disastrous arrogance is to be less to ourselves than the Lord has been.

Speak to yourself now in the quiet of your own heart. Say your name. "_____, I forgive you as one forgiven by the Lord."

Now you are ready for a releasing freedom. Jesus did more than forgive the woman. He told her to go and sin no more. How would she accomplish that? Only if her self-condemnatory spirit had been healed by the Lord's forgiving Spirit.

Paul said, "Stand fast therefore in the liberty by which Christ has made us free, and do not be entangled again with a yoke of bondage" (Galatians 5:1). A new yoke of slavery is offered every day by life's temptations and challenges. So how can we be free?

We do what we do because of what we are inside. Until those needs are met creatively, we will continue to be constantly vulnerable. We all need a new image of ourselves: Christ's picture of us—a portrait of a loved and accepted person. Until His love possesses and pervades us, we will seek to use people and things as substitutes.

The sure test that we have accepted the Lord's image of us as forgiven is that we begin to feel good about ourselves. A new dignity and self-worth will replace the negative self-depreciation. Self-hate is the prelude to all the things we do that cause us to despise ourselves.

The formula works. Allow Christ to love you; dare to love yourself as an accepted, forgiven person. He is more concerned about our reclamation than recrimination!

Now is the only moment we have. It is the first moment of our new future. Start where you stand!

There is a lovely story of a man who asked an older man in a little village what the seemingly insignificant wide place in the road was known for. "Young man," the villager responded, "this is the starting place for any place in the world. You can start from here and go anywhere you want to."

In a way, that is what Jesus Christ says to us right now. Feel his strong arms lift you up when you are down on yourself. "Neither do I condemn you. Go and sin no more!" That is all we need to know. We are forgiven, free to forget, and released to live without self-condemnation. The fruit of the kindness of the Lord will be manifested in kindness to others.

William Penn said, "I expect to pass through life but once. If, therefore, there be any kindness I can show, or any good thing I can do to my fellow-beings, let me do it now and not defer it, as I shall not pass this way again."

One of the most effective ways to nurture the growth of the fruit of kindness, true graciousness, is to take a prolonged time for quiet reflection with pen and paper in hand. Draw a line down the center of the page. On the left side list the times the Lord forgave you and gave you the power to forgive yourself. When you finish this list take time to praise Him for all the undeserved grace you have received.

Now on the right side of your sheet of paper list the people to whom you need to express kindness in gracious forgiveness. Be specific. Put down the hurts, the slights and oversights, the painful memories that fester inside you. Whose forgiveness do you need to receive? Whom do you need to forgive?

It's helpful to keep this inventory sheet handy. When you have acted out your forgiveness, put a check beside the items on the right side of the page. When all have been done, burn the sheet. You are free!

Having What It Takes

You can never be "good enough" on your own to please God. Only the Holy Spirit has what it takes to give us what it takes to please God: His essential goodness reproduced in us.

Having What It Takes

A FEW YEARS AGO I conducted the funeral of a very outstanding man. After the service, I accompanied the family to the cemetery. The hearse pulled up near the grave, and I took my place with the pallbearers to lead the procession. As we moved along past the gravestones, I was deeply engrossed in my memories of the man whose body we were about to bury. I felt the loss of this man who expressed the goodness of God in his life.

Reflecting on this, I was shocked by the arrogant words of an old tombstone beside the path. It marked the grave of a man buried years before. I almost stopped in my tracks.

What kind of a man would have that kind of a gravestone, with that kind of an epitaph? Chiseled in granite were these words: "Here lies a man who had what it takes."

What it takes for what? To live a full and abundant life? To be a success? To be powerful? To live a rich and creative life that makes a difference? To be a good person? Did God agree that the man represented by that gravestone had exemplified what it takes?

I talked to a woman who was deeply depressed. She had a very difficult life. Her husband had left her and later came back for a weekend. During the visit he secretly packed the children's clothes, and, when she was away at the grocery store, he took the children. She had no way of knowing where they were. She looked at me with tears streaming down her face and said, "Lloyd, I just don't have what it takes!"

A man wrote to me about an awesome challenge he had been given. The opportunity was immense. He felt inadequate and insecure. In the letter he confessed, "If only I were good enough and had what it takes!"

If we are to have what it takes, it will mean that we allow the Lord to work His very nature into the fabric of our character. It is His plan to do this. He is ready to implant His Spirit into the very substance of our personalities. We have discussed the resulting character traits of love, joy, peace, patience, kindness. We are now ready to talk about goodness.

The fruit of the Spirit is goodness.

Without goodness we cannot have what it takes to please God or to accomplish our purpose in being alive. Goodness is the secret of really succeeding in life.

But what is goodness?

THE WORD EVERYONE USES
AND NO ONE DEFINES

We'd agree with nineteenth-century preacher, Henry Ward Beecher, who said, "Goodness is a very composite word that everybody uses and nobody defines."

We exclaim, "Oh, for goodness' sake!" as a kind of thoughtless expression in response to things both glad and sad. At Christmastime, children are tunefully challenged to be "good for goodness' sake." We would be hard-pressed to answer if a child asked, "What's goodness?" Our answer would probably focus on the child's behavior and obedience. Most people's notion of goodness is related to agreeable behavior or flawless morality. God's idea of goodness is concerned with something much more than that.

Goodness is the generosity God defines. If we would understand goodness we must look to the nature of God. Goodness is a metonymn for God, one of the attributes that often serves as one of His names.

Again we go back to Mount Sinai to listen to what God has said about Himself. Moses pled with God, "Please show me Your glory." God's answer was, "I will make all My goodness pass before you, and I will proclaim the name of the Lord before you. I will be gracious to whom I will be gracious, and I will have compassion on whom I will have compassion" (Exodus 33:18-19).

There, for openers, is the essence of goodness: it is synonymous with God's glory, the manifestation of His presence in outrushing, generous love poured out in graciousness and compassion. When we attest that God is good, we affirm that He is always consistent, never changes, constantly fulfills His purpose, and is totally dependable. We sing with Thomas Chisholm, "O God my Father! There is no shadow of turning with Thee; Thou changest not, Thy compassions, they fail not: as Thou hast been Thou forever wilt be."

When God created the world and all aspects of it, He

reviewed His work and concluded, "It is good." At the end of the sixth day of creation, He formed a human being, and then He said, "It is very good."

Nothing is complicated about the use of the word in the Hebrew text. It means that all of the aspects of creation are ready to fulfill their purpose. The plant life, the seas, the fish that swim in the seas, the animals that roam the plains, and the sublime level of His creation, human beings, are all able to function as they were intended. All are good.

Now all of creation is to be a glory to God and a manifestation of His goodness to fulfill His purpose. Our essential purpose is to glorify God and to enjoy Him forever. Insofar as "all creatures great and small" keep a life consistent with the basic reason for which they exist, goodness is maintained.

We know all too well what happened, but Adam and Eve did not lose their "good" rating just because they did a lot of bad things. Evil entered their hearts. They envied God's control over them. They wanted to control their own lives and did so by refusing to be faithful to the conditions of obedience; they denied their goodness in rebellion against God.

But God will not cease to be good. He brooded over His flawed creation. The biblical account of history reveals Him persistently seeking to bring humankind back to what He had intended—good, open to Him, obedient to His guidance, trusting in His faithfulness, generous. And good people stand out on the pages of Genesis—Enoch, Noah, Abraham, Isaac, Jacob, and Joseph—all good because they eventually fulfilled their purpose of glorifying God and obeying His will in spite of their initial resistance.

Then God made one of His many big moves. He elected Moses to be the liberator and led His people out of Egypt, revealing His goodness in graciousness and compassion. The Commandments were graciously given to guide His people in goodness, in fulfilling their purpose in being faithful and obedient to Him.

The goodness of God was expressed in His magnificent generosity to His people. Each time the word *goodness* is used for God in the biblical accounts of His blessings on Israel, it flashes with praise for His tremendous generosity.

David could not contain his adoration for God's goodness. Psalm 27 records his prayer in the midst of difficult circumstances. His enemies were all around him. But those circumstantial facts were quite secondary in David's focus. "I would have lost heart, unless I had believed that I would see the goodness of the Lord in the land of the living" (v. 13).

That led to the confident trust we noted earlier. "Wait on the Lord; be of good courage, and He shall strengthen your heart; wait I say on the Lord!" (v. 14). David trusted his divine rear-guard, "Surely *goodness* and mercy shall follow me all the days of my life" (Psalm 23:6). He was confident that "the goodness of God endures continually" (Psalm 52:1).

Perhaps one of the greatest passages in the Old Testament recounting the goodness of God is Psalm 107. The frequent repetition of the words, "Oh, that men would give thanks to the Lord for His goodness" stirs our minds to think magnificently about God's generosity. If you were to write a psalm of praise for His generosity, what would you list as evidences of His goodness to you? Surely your praise would include the most awesome expression of His goodness. It's not in the list of wonderful works in Psalm 107. The prophets longed for it and predicted it with awesome precision.

THE STUNNING GOODNESS OF GOD

God's goodness, the ultimate expression of His generosity, was that at a time when humankind deserved it the least, He came in Jesus Christ to reveal His goodness incarnate and to die for the sins of the whole race. The glory of God, consummate goodness, stunning generosity, was revealed on Calvary. *He came to give us what it takes—to make men and women like us good from the inside.*

Goodness is an inside story. We are made good not by our efforts but by the efficacy of the atonement accomplished by Jesus Christ on the Cross. Our status before God is in and through Christ. He accepts us as new creatures, made good on Golgotha. We could not dare to come to God apart from the imputed goodness of our standing mediated through the Savior. The Lord looks at us through the focused lens of Calvary. Our confidence is not in our human facsimiles of goodness, but in our relationship with Christ. We are freed from compulsive efforts to be good enough to deserve love. Instead, we can live in the settled security of God's generosity, manifested in the goodness of Christ.

Paul confronts this issue in Romans, chapter three. He quotes portions of Psalm 14 and 53 in establishing what we are like apart from Christ. "There is none righteous, no, not one; there is none who understands; there is none who seeks after God. They have all gone out of the way.... There is none who does good, no, not one" (Romans 3:10-12). The apostle goes on to assert that no one will be justified, made good, by works. Then he thunders the essential truth: "But now the righteousness of God apart from the law is revealed... even the righteousness of God, which is through faith in Jesus Christ to all and on all who believe" (Romans 3:21-22).

GOODNESS IS A GIFT

To be sure we get the point that our goodness is in Christ, Paul restates the case. "For there is no difference; for all have sinned and fall short of the glory of God, being justified freely by His grace through the redemption that is in Christ Jesus, whom God set forth to be a propitiation by His blood through faith, to demonstrate His righteousness because in His forbearance God had passed over the sins that were previously committed to demonstrate at the present time His righteousness that He might be just and the justifier of the one who has faith in Jesus" (Romans 3:22-26).

Our goodness in Christ is a gift. We accept it by faith and then are released to live in the flow of His goodness—to and through us. On the basis of that we can respond to Paul's challenge to "overcome evil with good" (Romans 12:21). And that is possible because our life will be guided by the Lord in each situation and relationship. "I appeal to you therefore, brethren, by the mercies of God, to present your bodies as a living sacrifice, holy and acceptable to God, which is your spiritual worship. Do not be conformed to this world but be transformed by the renewal of your mind, that you may prove what is the will of God, what is good and acceptable and perfect" (Romans 12:1-2).

So the goodness of God gives us *what it takes* to please Him. Through the Cross our status as loved, forgiven, redeemed people has been settled now and for eternity. But that's not all. There's more, much more. Out of unqualified goodness, we are given the gift of the indwelling Spirit of Christ. The goodness of God in Jesus' character can be transplanted into us. We are not only made good through Christ; we are empowered to communicate goodness to others. *We are given what it takes for our relationships.*

The Greek word Paul used for the fruit of goodness is the noun *agathosune*. Like the adjective for good, *agathos*, it means a particular quality of goodness. It is goodness that is outgoing and beneficial in its effect. Another word for good, *kalos*, emphasizes the intrinsic good of a thing or person, whereas *agathos* stresses *initiative good*. Also, *agathos* and *agathosune* were the most frequently used Greek words for *good* and *goodness* in the Septuagint, the Greek translation of the Old Testament, published before Christ.* Paul would have been conversant with the Septuagint. Since *agathosune* was a peculiarly biblical word known to Paul through his readings of the

---

* Kittle states that the Rabbinical confession regarding Ps. 27:13 is, "The perfectly good being of God which consists in His goodness... The idea of good in the Greek or Hellenistic sense is not present. *Agathosune* comes down from the Septuagint into the New Testament... the Christian's radically new possibility of life... the possession of which constitutes the content of the life of the Christian (Rom. 15:14). It is best understood as 'love' which the Christian is enabled to exercise... 'the good' is achieved in concrete I-Thou relationships" (Vol., p.13, 16).

Septuagint, his use of it for a fruit of the Spirit is very significant. He clearly uses it as an attribute of God imputed in our character by the Spirit of Christ.

In the parable of the laborers (Matthew 20:1-16), the word *agathos*, good, is used in a revealing way. You will remember that the landowner needed laborers to harvest his vineyard, and hired them at dawn, nine in the morning, noon, three, and five in the afternoon. One of the laborers, who had been promised a denarius for his day's labor, was dismayed that all the others hired later in the day were paid the same amount. The response of the landowner was, "Friend, I am doing you no wrong; did you not agree with me for a denarius? Take what is yours and go your way, but I wish to give this last man the same as you. Is it not lawful for me to do what I wish with what is my own? Or is your eye envious because I am generous?" (Matthew 20:13-16, RSV). *The New King James Bible* has it, "because I am good." F.F. Bruce comments, "'Is your eye evil because I am good (*agathos*)'... where 'generosity' is precisely what *agathos* means."

The landowner in Jesus' parable represents God, who is generous in His love. This is the same generosity expressed in Jesus' promise, "Give and it will be given to you; good measure, pressed down, shaken together, and running over will be put into your bosom. For with the measure that you use, it will be measured back to you" (Luke 6:38).

GOODNESS IS AN ACTIVE BLESSING

The fruit of goodness is an active quality that enables us to be vigorously involved to bless, encourage, uplift, and bring out the best in others. This kind of goodness is not a passive possession, but is expressed in affirmation of the value of others, lifting of burdens, practical caring, and unstinting use of our time, energy, and money to help others become all that God meant them to be. The fruit of the Spirit of goodness makes us truly generous.

Other than here in the fruit of the Spirit, Paul uses *agathosune* in only three other places. In Ephesians 5:8-10 it is one of the character traits of those who walk in the light. "For you were once darkness, but now you are light in the Lord. Walk as children of light (for the fruit of the Spirit is in all goodness, righteousness, and truth) proving what is acceptable to the Lord." In the light of Christ, we see what true goodness is and claim the goodness of His Spirit in us.

GOODNESS WORKS HAND IN HAND WITH KNOWLEDGE

Romans 15:13-14 helps us to know how the fruit of goodness can be expressed in our relationships. Paul reminds the Christians in Rome what God's goodness has meant to them and then affirms the endowed character trait of goodness in them. "Now may the God of hope fill you with joy and hope in believing, that you may abound in hope by the power of the Holy Spirit. Now I myself am confident concerning you, my brethren, that you also are full of goodness, filled with all knowledge, able to admonish one another."

That's quite a compliment! We are thankful these Spirit-filled disciples had motivated Paul to applaud their willingness to be a blessing to others. What he wrote shows us how the fruit of the Spirit of goodness works in harmony with the gift of the Spirit of knowledge making us effective in our ministry of encouragement to others.

Here's how it works. When the Spirit lives in us, we're given the character trait of goodness, the generous desire to care for others and their needs. But without discerning knowledge of the problems and potential of people, we can be inept and ineffective. The spiritual gift of knowledge gives us supernatural insight. We are given X-ray vision into people and what the Lord wants us to say and do. If we are open and receptive, the Spirit will give us the gift of knowledge to meet the need before us. Like all the gifts listed in 1 Corinthians, chapter twelve, the gift of knowledge is neither an exclusive gift of some, nor a permanent gift of any. It is equipment for ministry given when we pray for it, and it guides the wise use of our endowed goodness. The gift of knowledge is not human scholarship or intellectual acumen. It is the Spirit giving us divine perception of what's going on beneath the surface of people and situations.

When the generosity of the fruit of goodness is coupled with the gift of knowledge, we are able to admonish one another. "Admonish" may seem like a rather stern word. Actually, the Greek verb *noutheteo* means "to put in mind." That makes us wonder what we register in people's minds: what image of themselves do we communicate? How do people think and feel about themselves after they have been with us? People need to know we believe in them, are for them, and will help them through their struggles. Advice or bracing challenges will be received only after we have communicated affirming love. We must win a person with the warmth of the Spirit's goodness before we can warn them. Paul describes the preparation required for really caring for people. "Let the word of Christ dwell in you richly in all wisdom, teaching and admonishing one another in psalms and hymns and spiritual songs, singing with grace in your hearts to the Lord" (Colossians 3:16).

"A GOODNESS TIME"

Often, I'm awakened early in the morning with the people challenges of the day ahead on my mind and heart. I know that I will not have what it will take to have a maximum day without the implanted fruit of goodness, the imparted gift of knowledge, and the inspired ability to help people focus in their minds what they can be with the Lord's power. What I do know from experience is that the Lord can give me what it takes.

So, I get out of bed and begin what I call "a goodness time." It starts with a review of the Scriptures about the goodness of the Lord. Some of those I have quoted in this chapter have been memorized through the years, so I say them or sing them out loud. Then I list the recent evidences of the Lord's goodness in my life. After that, I reclaim the fruit of Christ's character, particularly the quality of goodness and the gift of knowledge. While I'm doing that I sing the words of the chorus, "God is so good, God is so good, He's so good to me." At this point, I pray individually for each of the people I will encounter that day, those on my appointment calendar and others the Lord will add in the surprises of the day. I ask for the flow of His goodness through me perfectly mingled with knowledge and the sensitivity to speak the truth in love.

My best days begin with this kind of quiet time with the Lord. And, you guessed it, my least effective days are those when I don't have what it takes because I didn't take time to open the floodgate of my heart to the inrush and outflow of the goodness of the Lord.

Robert Louis Stevenson said, "There is an idea abroad among moral people that they should make their neighbors good. One person I have to make good: myself." I agree with the great Scot that we can't make people good—only the Lord can do that. But I disagree with the notion that we can make ourselves good. When we can yield to the growth of the fruit of goodness, we can have what it takes.

The Lord gets inside of us. He takes the tangled mess of our memories, of what we have done or said that we never should have done or said. He takes all the confused relationships, the fantasies and the fears, and He forgives them. He deals redemptively with our guilt and cleanses and heals us because He is good—and He created us to be good.

So the idea that goodness is obtained by a pious withdrawal from ungodly persons for fear of contamination is false. Our admonitions to people, "Try and be good," and eulogies like, "Here was a really good person," are comforting, but usually wide of the mark of true goodness. Christ-imputed goodness can be attributed only to someone who trusts Him and is filled with His Spirit, to someone who dares in all things to trust Him for direction, guidance, and the impartation of His own nature.

The church fathers put it this way: "God is a Spirit, infinite, eternal, and unchangeable, in His being (in His essential nature), wisdom, power, holiness, justice, goodness, and truth" (*The Shorter Catechism*).

It is possible to treasure such a profound declaration to the point where it becomes a revered document instead of a truth to be realized and appropriated. *Christ wants to make us like Himself.* When the Holy Spirit takes residence in us, He makes us consistent, authentic, real persons. We become good and are able to see the right and do it, motivated by His love. We sense the needs of others, and without being told, we respond with mercy.

God has been good to us so that we may be good people. His goodness within us can be constant. Even now, in the quiet, do you feel it? Do you sense it? Have you ever thought of the wonder of being shaped in the image of the goodness of Christ? He longs to live His life, develop His character, and love His world through you. Inadvertently, winsomely, naturally, freely—His goodness will grow in you and become part of your own character. Hugh Latimer was right: "We must first be made good before we can do good." Goodness is not just what we do but the inward good person we become through the reconciliation of the Cross and the infilling of the fruit of the Spirit.

Then we can say with the psalmist, "Surely goodness and mercy shall follow me all the days of my life" (Psalm 23:6). I have often wondered why he said "follow me." Could it be that he meant the Lord takes care of the enemies which attack us from behind? There are enemies of our yesterdays which can attack and rob us of our birthright of goodness in the present. Memories dog our steps; past sins are forever on our heels. We move forward, but the relentless fears of the past persist. Then the Lord becomes our rear guard as well as our advance guard. We know we will "dwell in the house of the Lord for ever," and we also know that the Lord's "goodness and mercy" stand between us and our yesterdays. He is Lord of the past, and Lord of the future, so that we can enjoy the "goodness" of companionship with Him today.

I am gratified that after I passed by the "Here lies a man who had what it takes" tombstone, I led the procession on to the open grave of the dear friend I was burying that day. We committed his body to the ground with the full assurance that he was alive in the house of the Lord. When the grave was closed, his marker was put in place. It gave his name, the years of his physical life on earth, and these powerful words, "To God be the glory." That is all a good person ever needs to say about yesterday, today, and tomorrow!

Through the fruit of goodness, we will *have what it takes* —for now and eternity. And day by day, we can sing the words of the old hymn,

I could not do without Thee
    I cannot stand alone,
I have no strength or goodness
    Nor wisdom of my own
But Thou, beloved Savior,
    Art all in all to me,
And perfect strength in weakness
    Is theirs who lean on Thee.

Whatever Happened to Faithfulness?

What if God was only faithful when he felt like it, only dependable part of the time, only loving on special occasions? Thank goodness, He is always faithful to His own nature. The world desperately needs to see that same kind of faithfulness in our lives.

Whatever Happened to Faithfulness?

I F YOU HAD TO SELECT one of the aspects of God's nature as His crowning attribute, what would it be? His love, mercy, goodness? Or would it be His sovereignty, omnipotence, or omniscience?

There's no doubt in my mind; I would say that the crowning attribute of God is His faithfulness.

Are you surprised? Allow me to explain: the faithfulness of God is His immutability, His unchangeableness, His constancy and consistency.

All the other attributes of God would set us up for a shattering disappointment if it were not for His faithfulness—His dependability. What if God loved only some of the time? Think what it would be like if He couldn't be counted on to be gracious in all circumstances. What if His goodness vacillated? Imagine a God who is moody, given to playing favorites, open to compromising His righteousness and justice. What a madhouse life would be!

But our confidence is that we can sing with Henry F. Lyte,

Swift to its close ebbs out life's little day;
Earth's joys grow dim, its glories pass away;
Change and decay in all around I see
O Thou who changest not abide with me.

And abide He does. He never acts out of character,
never is less than His grace, and never contradicts His
own nature. God will always love us; He stands by His
covenant; His promises are sure. This is the dominant
note of the Bible: God's persistent loyalty to His revealed
nature—and to us. John Donne put it this way, "One of
the most convenient hieroglyphics of God is a circle,
and a circle is endless; who God loves, He loves to the
end; and not only to their own end, to their death, but
to His end; and His end is that He might love them still."
That constancy is our confidence, as Samuel Rutherford
said it so well, "Often and often, I have in my folly torn
up my own copy of God's covenant with me; but blessed
be His name, He keeps the principal in heaven safe, and
He stands by it always."

GOD IS RELENTLESSLY FAITHFUL

God's faithfulness is rooted in His holiness. He is what
He is, magnificently and sublimely so. What Sherlock
Holmes said of his friend Watson we can say of God with
no fear of human fallibility, "You are my one fixed point
in a world of change." God is our ultimate point-person
because He is the same today as He was in the beginning. We can count on God's faithfulness *always.*

Always? "That's an almighty word!" you say. Indeed it

is. We can safely use it only for the Almighty who consistently employs His power to bless us and, in spite of
everything, bring us into relationship with Him. He is
faithful, regardless of what we do to ourselves or what
life dishes out. Even in the calamities of our free but
fallen world, God works relentlessly to reach us, bringing
good out of our worst mistakes and the diabolical strate-
gies of evil. Only God can say, "I will always love you!"
and never fail to follow though in a way that brings
about our ultimate good and reveals His glory.

In the Old Testament, God's faithfulness is synonymous with His reliability and steadfastness. This crowning attribute of God was affirmed in times of affliction.
The psalmist's praise in Psalm 89 was based on the sure
rock of God's faithfulness to His promises and covenant.
"I will sing of the mercies of the Lord forever; with my
mouth will I make known your faithfulness to all generations" (v. 1). The word "faithfulness" is used at least six
times in the psalm. It was also on the tip of the tongue of
God's people in trying times. It was a battle cry in confronting their enemies. And even when the glory of
Israel was diminished through apostasy and syncretism
with other gods, the prophets stuck to their conviction
that judgment is a part of the holy faithfulness of God. It
cannot be otherwise. He created His people to be faithful to Him. And so, in Hosea, we feel the pulse beat of
unbroken love from God's broken heart. "Ephraim is
joined to idols, let him alone" (Hosea 4:17). But that's
not the final word. "How can I give you up, Ephraim?
How can I hand you over, Israel?" (Hosea 11:8). It was
out of faithful love that the Lord both condemned what
stood between Him and His people, and kept His faith-

ful promise to restore them after their exile.

Even when Jerusalem fell in the southern kingdom, Jeremiah would not give up his dogged assurance of God's faithfulness. "This I will call to mind, therefore I have hope. Through the Lord's mercies we are not consumed, because His compassions fail not. They are new every morning; great is Your faithfulness" (Lamentations 3:21-23).

The faithfulness of God, His crowning attribute, was the sure foundation of the hope that vibrated in the hearts of the prophets as they looked forward to the time God would send the Messiah. When Isaiah thundered the promise of the Messiah, it followed the lightning flash of assurance, "Because of the Lord who is faithful" (Isaiah 49:7).

And so Immanuel, God with us, came in search of His own. From the lips of this pursuing, relentless, indefatigable Savior flowed the unforgettable images of faithfulness. What is faithfulness? A father who would never give up on his younger son in the far country of rebellion or an elder son in the near country of self-righteousness; a shepherd who goes in search of a lost sheep; a merchantman who sells everything to purchase the pearl of great price. God in search of His own, saying "I cannot let you go!"

Again we come to the foot of the Cross, the place where the attributes of God flash forth with radiance. Calvary was, and will always be, the place to behold the faithfulness of God. He could deny neither His righteousness nor His grace.

This faithfulness never ceased to amaze the apostle Paul. Near the end of his life, in prison, the apostle encouraged Timothy to endure difficulties. The faithfulness of God in Christ was to be the young leader's strength. "If we are faithless, He remains faithful; He cannot deny Himself" (2 Timothy 2:13).

That is the best definition of faithfulness we can find: the Lord cannot deny Himself. He must be true to His nature; He will never contradict His promises; He will always be consistent. We can depend on His assurance, "I will always love you." Even when we are faithless, shake our fist at Him in rebellion, or turn on our heels and try to run away from Him, He is faithful. And because He is, all the other aspects of His nature—love, joy, peace, patience, kindness, and goodness—never fail. It sustained the apostle Paul to the end. He could attest to his own faithfulness because of the faithfulness of Christ to him, "I have fought the good fight, I have finished the race, I have kept the faith" (2 Timothy 4:7). All because the Lord's faithfulness had been implanted into his character; the crowning attribute of the Lord had been cloned in the apostle Paul.

The fruit of the Spirit is faithfulness.

THE COURAGE TO BE FAITHFUL

If, indeed, faithfulness is the crowning attribute of the Lord, then it must be the crowning fruit of the Spirit in us. It is the fruit that gives consistency and constancy to the expression of all the others. Implanted faithfulness makes us dependable. The Lord's faithfulness is that He cannot deny Himself. When His Spirit lives in us, He seeks to give us the courage not to deny Him or the new

134 / The Magnificent Vision

character traits He is nurturing in us.

If we have been amazed by the promise that the character of Christ can be established in us, we are also astonished by the offer that His faithfulness can be reproduced in us! "Consistent and constant like Christ in the expression of love, joy, peace, patience, kindness, goodness?" You question with wonderment. "That's simply beyond me!"

Well, you're right—it is beyond you, if "beyond you" means it exceeds your natural ability. We're all one in that—it's difficult to be faithful on our own. But from beyond us the Spirit comes within us. He gives us the gifts of the two kinds of faith.

First, we are empowered to say, "Jesus is Lord"—and mean it (1 Corinthians 12:3)! Then He gives us power to envision and claim what the Lord wants to do in and around us. Primary faith is augmented by the gift of practical faith for daily living (1 Corinthians 12:9). The Spirit within us paints on the picture screen of our imaginations what it will be like for us to love, experience joy, know peace, be patient, express kindness, and give ourselves away generously. More than that, the Spirit constantly reminds us that we are now creatures with a new character and that He will enable us to live the fruit He is producing in us. Remember that the Lord's faithfulness means He cannot deny Himself. The faithfulness He nurtures in us is to not deny Himself in us. So here's the glorious secret of faithfulness—"The Spirit Himself bears witness with our spirit that we are children of God, and if children, then heirs—heirs of God and joint heirs with Christ, if we suffer with Him, that we may also be glorified together" (Romans 8:16-17).

The indwelling Spirit reorients our thinking about who we are. We are chosen and cherished children of God, elected to be remade in the image of Christ and joint recipients of an inheritance. He assures us that we are to receive and transmit the fruit we've talked about in the preceding chapters. The fruit is our amazing new self. Let me say it again: faithfulness is being true to our new self, being consistent and constant in the expression of our inheritance of a Christlike character.

Now let's be very specific: where in your life do you find it most difficult to express the fruit of love, joy, peace, patience, kindness, and goodness? In what relationships and responsibilities are you tempted to contradict your new self and be inconsistent in your attitudes or behavior? Who tests the fruit of love in you? What can rob you of consistent joy? When are you most apt to panic and deny Christ's peace? Who or what makes you impatient? What blocks the kindness of forgiveness for yourself and others? When does selfishness keep you from generous goodness? In other words, when do you act out of character with your new character?

Then, too, times of difficulty, adversity, pressure and conflict show us how much we need the fruit of faithfulness—consistency and constancy. Physical or emotional pain sometimes causes us to act as if the Lord had forgotten us; rejection shows us how much we depend on people rather than the Lord; denial of our convictions because of criticism is an ever-present temptation.

Whatever happened to faithfulness? Here's my answer: faithfulness has been an *ought we taught* rather than a *power we sought*. Trying to be faithful on our own strength leads to either self-righteousness or defeatism.

Preaching and teaching faithfulness without identifying it as a fruit of the Spirit, an implanted character trait, may goad people to try harder, but it will also create a great deal of guilt. Pretending they are consistent, people will hide their inconsistencies, or they will express passive resistance to an authority figure who has communicated an inadequate motivation for loyalty to him or her.

FOUR PRINCIPLES OF FAITHFULNESS

Here are four basic truths I use to keep thinking clearly about true faithfulness.

1. Faithfulness is motivated by love. It never exists in a vacuum independent from a love relationship. We desire to be faithful, consistent in our loyalty to someone who has loved us and demonstrated that love. It's true for our relationship with our parents, our friends, and those who would lead us, but sublimely so in our relationship with God. He has demonstrated His faithfulness in His grace—unmerited, unlimited, unrestrained love. And we can count on the fact that He will never change. We learn what faithfulness is all about by God's relentless faithfulness to His covenant, His loving interventions to bless us, and His persistent determination in never giving up on us.

2. Faithfulness is the result of forgiveness. It is one thing to be told that God loves us, but we experience His faithfulness especially when we fail. There is nothing we can do that will make God stop loving us. To be sure, God judges us and arranges circumstances to break our pride

and call us to return to Him, but, as we've said, He cannot deny Himself—He remains faithful even when we
are faithless. John was constantly overwhelmed by God's
faithfulness—"If we confess our sins, He is faithful and
just to forgive us our sins and to cleanse us from all
unrighteousness" (1 John 1:9). As Arthur John Gossip
used to put it, "God's love is a sun that never sets, and
never sinks, is always, always at its full noonday glory! He
can never fall below His best, He cannot be untrue to
His own nature."

3. *Faithfulness is impossible without our own Pentecost.* Don't
miss the fact that the followers of Christ were unfaithful
until *after* He baptized them with the Holy Spirit. They
denied the Lord, deserted Him at the time of the
Crucifixion, and defected from discipleship. Even after
the Resurrection they vacillated, doubted, and were
powerless to be faithful to the Lord. But Christ did not
drum them out of the corps. He knew that faith*less*ness
was a natural human reaction. Only after the disciples
were filled with the power of the Spirit would they be
able to be faithful witnesses. But look at them after
Pentecost! Faithfulness became one of their distinguish-
ing qualities. They were amazing new creations, for the
first time able to be consistent in their loyalty. Living the
Lord's commandments was no grim, dutiful obligation;
it became a love-motivated delight.

The role of the Spirit is to empower us to know and
do the Father's will. He is the Spirit of faithfulness and
shows us how to be faithful in our prayers, obedient in
living the commandments and the moral and ethical
mandates of the Master, and do what love demands in
our relationships. His assignment in us is to display to

the world around us that faithfulness has not gone out of style. He wants to produce people who don't give up on others, who become involved in their suffering, who forgive when they fail, who are not put off by their personal weaknesses, and who affirm their potential when they find it difficult to believe in themselves.

4. Faithfulness is a fruit to behold. It is the first of the last triad of fruit that is produced in us for our witness. Just as the first triad is the fruit of our relationship to God, and the second is the fruit for our relationship with others, the last triad is so that we can be an example to others of what abiding in Christ and allowing Him to abide in us can mean for them.

In a world where faithfulness is woefully lacking, ours will be stunning and startling. Our consistency, loyalty, and reliability will stand out in bold contrast to what people have grown to expect. They will know that we mean it when we say, "You can count on me!" We can say that because the Spirit of faithfulness will never allow us to forget the faithfulness of God to us. And He will persistently work within us to keep us consistent. All so that when people have tested our faithfulness to the utmost, we will be given an opportunity to share the Source of our strength.

Whatever happened to faithfulness? It's still the crowning attribute of God, the character of His Son, and the undeniable trait of those in whom the Spirit lives: people like you and me, in whom the fruit of faithfulness is mysteriously, persistently growing.

NINE

The Power of Gentleness

Contrary to popular opinion, it takes strength to be gentle. To be truly gentle or meek means that we are no longer ruled by pride or defensiveness. We know who we are—and Whose we are!

The Power of Gentleness

THERE IS A STEREOTYPE for meekness in our culture that is anything but attractive. It is a Milquetoast kind of person whose only vocal contribution is the sound of the throat being cleared for speech that never comes.

If you have bought this stereotype, it may come as a distinct shock to you to know that meekness or gentleness is a characteristic of God that the Spirit can implant and wants to develop in you. God wants to make us His meek and gentle people who can display His power.

In Paul's inventory of the fruit of the Spirit, the King James Version translates this quality as meekness, but it means something quite different from the weakness often associated with the word. *Gentleness* is a far better word. It is an essential part of God's fatherly grace that He wants modeled by us, His own children.

I remember hearing a marvelous story about Alexander the Great. A child he had sired grew to manhood and joined his father's army. In one of the battles he acted in a cowardly manner and was brought before the commanding general. Alexander did not recognize his own son. The demands of military life had kept him from associating with the boy as he grew. He did know, however, that he was looking into the face of a coward. The charge was justified. The account was true.

Alexander looked him squarely in the eye and said, "Young man, what is your name?"

"A... Al... Alexander, sir," the boy stuttered.

Alexander the Great said a second time, "Young man, what is your name?"

"A... Al... Alexander, sir," was the response.

And then, reviewing the young man's cowardly act, Alexander took him by the shoulders and shook him and said, "Change your character, or change your name!"

There is an inescapable message here for us. If we call ourselves Christians, we need to have the character imprint of God and His Son upon us. We need to change our character—or change our name.

The fruit of the Spirit is gentleness.

I was forcibly reminded of that one day when a chain of highly irritating, and, in my mind, grossly unnecessary mechanical problems immobilized my car on the corner of Gower Street and Sunset Boulevard. Already behind for an appointment, I called the auto club. Two hours and not one, but two, auto club trucks later, my car finally started. I was in a turbulent mood as I headed back up Gower Street on my way to Glendale for my belated speaking engagement. I was thinking of all the ways I could express my frustration in a letter to the president of the auto club, when I caught a glimpse of the marquee of my own church announcing the next Sunday's sermon title the Lord had given me a whole year before: "In God's Name, Be Gentle!" I needed that admonition more than the people who would hear the sermon on gentleness. But then, God often gives me a fresh experience of what I am planning to preach.

AUTHENTIC GENTLENESS

There is no other way to be gentle than by the name and power the Lord gives us. Authentic gentleness is one of the most miraculous manifestations of the inner power of Christ's indwelling. It requires absolute trust in His ongoing work in others. It responds to the wonder of what people have been through, not to what they have done. It addresses the emerging child, often hurt and battered, in other people.

The Lord is consistently gentle with us. He stands beside us in the midst of trouble and tragedy, nursing us through it all. That is the same kind of encouragement the people around us need.

What does it mean to be gentle in life's tensions and problems? It certainly does not mean simply having a soft, easy lack of concern. Moses was referred to as one of the meekest men in all of Israel, and yet he martialed the mass exodus of a diverse company of people and brought them through the wilderness to the promised land.

But it is in Jesus Christ that we see gentleness in its true light. Though the word is not used, the passage which shows us true gentleness is the account of the Passover feast in the thirteenth chapter of John's Gospel. "Jesus, knowing that the Father had given all things into His hands, and that He had come from God and was going to God, rose from supper and laid aside His garments, took a towel and girded Himself. After that, He poured water into a basin, and began to wash the disciples' feet" (John 13:3-5). Jesus knew who He was and what He had come to do. He could do the servant's work. His life and death portray gentleness. He loved His enemies and followers alike, those who deceived Him, betrayed Him, and crucified Him. He was totally free of defensiveness.

The same character that was in Christ can be in us. I wonder if that is the reason why the French, in the translation of this beatitude, "Blessed are the meek..." used the word *debonaire*. For the French that means winsome and free, because the person knows the source of his or her power.

But let's press on. The word *praotēs* from *praus* in Greek has a profound implication for us. For Aristotle, it stood for the mean point between too much anger and too little anger, a point between over-expression and under-expression. A meek or gentle person was one who was under such control that he or she was able to express the reality of each emotion without excess.

There is more. The word *praus,* as I mentioned earlier, describes an animal which has been brought under the reins or control of a master and is now guidable. The truly meek are those who have gone through an experience when their arrogant self-will has been broken. They have come to a place of deep humility. *Praus* in Greek is the opposite of *huperēphania.* Pride is always contrasted with humility. It is holding oneself above others instead of caring for others guided by the control of the Master's reins.

When we are truly meek, we know who we are because we know to Whom we belong. We do not have to be defensive or justify ourselves any longer. We know we are loved and are therefore free to love and free to be the unique, special, unreproduceable wonders that God meant us to be. Once the defensive pride is taken from us by an authentic experience of humility, we are able to treat others as God has treated us.

I was fascinated as I studied the word *meekness* (or *gentleness*) in many different biblical settings and found it to be a relational word. It deals with the correction of one Christian by another and how to treat persons in the midst of problems.

After Paul has listed the fruit or characteristics of the Spirit to the Galatians, he is quoted in the sixth chapter as saying: "Brethren, if a man is overtaken in any trespass, you who are spiritual should restore him in a spirit of gentleness, considering yourself lest you also be tempted" (6:1). It is out of a recognition of our own inadequacy that we can be tender toward others.

I read a newspaper account of a speech reportedly given by the outspoken atheist, Madalyn Murray O'Hair. Her audience of young people listened patiently as she gave her speech opposing religion in American life and her deprecation of God and faith. When she concluded, a young woman stood up and spoke with gentle purpose. She thanked Ms. O'Hair for coming to speak and told her that the young people had listened with attention. Then she thanked her for showing them what an atheist really is and she expressed gratitude to her for strengthening their beliefs by her attack. Then she told her how sorry they were for her. Again she thanked her for coming and said they now had even more love and faith in

God as a result of seeing what life without God would be.

There is meekness in defense of the faith! Meekness that has strength. In the deafening applause that followed the girl's words, Ms. O'Hair left the platform.

THE SECRET OF BLESSEDNESS

Meekness should be the basis of receiving the word of God. James says, "Therefore lay aside all filthiness and overflow of wickedness, and receive with meekness the implanted word, which is able to save your souls" (James 1:21).

James has given us the secret in the word *receive*. True meekness or gentleness is receptivity. We cannot give away what we have not received. Nor can we receive all that God wants to give us unless we give away what is given to us for others. This is the magnificent meaning of the third beatitude. The gentle inherit the earth. They are the blessed. Note the progression in the beatitude. Blessed means beloved, belonging to God, cherished, called, and chosen. Those who know their sublime status are able to be gentle, completely open to what God wants to give, and sensitive to His guidance. Because they are, they can inherit the earth. The phrase has its roots in Psalm 37:11, "But the meek shall inherit the earth and shall delight themselves in the abundance of peace."

To the Hebrews, it meant first the promised land, then the providence of God, and finally the fulfillment of the Messianic age. Surely the latter was on Jesus' mind when He gave this secret of blessedness. All that He had come to be and do would be available to those who were receptive. His nature would be implanted and His power unleashed in them. Paul underlined this when he called us "joint-heirs with Christ" (Romans 8:17). Our inheritance was sealed on Calvary, assured on Easter, and completed on Pentecost. Meekness is being open to the new and fresh thing the Lord wants to give so that we can become channels of His grace to others.

Now look at the results. Catch the power and significance if you will. The meek shall eat and be satisfied. Jesus will guide the meek to abundant peace. He will teach them His way.

We inherit the earth because we are children of the Father, and everything that is His belongs to us. When His nature is in us, we become free to be gentle, free to love because our Father's love has healed our personalities. We know we are God's children and are free to be that with abandonment. "Behold what manner of love the Father has bestowed on us, that we should be called children of God! Beloved, now we are children of God; it has not yet been revealed what we shall be, but we know that when He appears we shall be like Him, for we shall see Him as He is" (1 John 3:1-2).

Far from being apologetic in manner, God's gentleness that we inherit is a mind-set that shapes and tempers the style of what we are as the people of God. Now on the basis of all that, we can allow the Lord to cure our future worries; activate the characteristic of gentleness implicit in your new heredity; become a gracious receiver. I am convinced that what God has done in the past is nothing in comparison with what He is ready to do. Now. Today. Trust Him.

The only time the future tense is used in a salutation or greeting in the epistles of the New Testament is in the second letter of John. He says: "Grace, mercy, and peace be with you from God the Father and from the Lord Jesus Christ" (2 John 3). That's the assurance I need. We are rooted in the very nature of God, in His plan for us, the way He works with us, and what happens inside us.

Gentleness is the key given to us to trust what God did in Jesus Christ as our Savior. That is a gift. And gentleness is also a spiritual muscle inherent in our new nature, waiting to be exercised to unlock the resources of the power of Christ to apply to our specific situations. Only that kind of inner strength is an antidote to anxiety. Only faith can cure our lack of trust. And as the nature of Christ begins to grow in us, we become identifiably gentle people.

How many people can you count on, really count on, to share your vision and the adventure? How many people are rocklike points of reference in your life?

I have a friend who calls me whenever he is alerted by God to the fact that I need a particular touch of grace. "Lloyd, I'm with you all the way!," he will say. And he has done that for thirty-five years.

So many of us are like mercury where our faith is concerned, so hesitant to connect our character to God's consistency. I know because I am often like that myself. Not long ago I found myself simultaneously faced with the payment of a horrendous tax bill and the fulfillment of a mission pledge. I looked at my checkbook and all of my assets and it was obvious I could not pay both of them. I was about to leave for a tour of our missionaries in the Orient, and I knew it would be hard to present myself as someone firmly behind missions if I had not paid my own pledge.

I went through the whole day with some uneasiness about the matter before I had time to open my folder of mail in my study. There was a check in that folder from a publisher for an amount I had not anticipated receiving. I did not know whether to laugh or cry, so I did both. It was for the exact amount I needed.

God is faithful. Because He is, we can be the gentle, meek people of the world. We can trust our future to Him.

TEN

Call Central Casting for the Real You

Do you believe that you are a unique never-to-be-repeated miracle? To be nobody but the person God created you to be is a battle, and it takes self-control to win it.

Call Central Casting
for the Real You

THE MOVIE COMPANIES in Hollywood have special departments called "central casting." They coordinate the selection of actors and actresses for parts in movie productions. "Call central casting... " is a familiar refrain of directors and producers when someone is needed for a particular part.

The other day, I visited a movie set where a member of my church was taking part in a scene of a forthcoming movie. While sitting on the sideline watching with great interest, I overheard a fascinating conversation.

A young actor came on the set to do a bit part. The director looked at him, sizing him up for the drama. "Who are you?" he asked insistently. The young man gave his name. "I don't want *your* name," the director replied, "What part are you playing?" The befuddled fledgling was not sure. I'll never forget the director's impatient response. "You'd better call central casting and find out who you are!"

You are probably ahead of me about the insight I got out of that exchange. Add a definite article to the director's command and you really have something. Call *the* central casting and find out who you are. In the drama of real life, our greatest challenge is to know who we are and be faithful to that person in every way. Only the ultimate casting director, the Lord Himself, can help us with that.

Each of us is a unique, never-to-be-repeated miracle. So often we deny that uniqueness by trying to contradict the real person we are inside. I think E.E. Cummings was right: "To be nobody but yourself in a world which is doing its best, night and day, to make you everybody else—means the hardest battle which any human being can fight and never stop fighting."

The last of the fruit of the Spirit gives us power to do just that. Self-control, the final jewel of the inner splendor mentioned under Paul's code name *fruit,* is the one which makes all the rest operative. To the Greek, self-control was to have "power over oneself." Paul grasped this quality from the four cardinal virtues of the Stoics and claimed it as one of the imputed vibrancies of the Holy Spirit. The Greek word, *egkrateia,* means holding control. It is often translated as temperance, as in the King James Version of the Bible. But since temperance is often used in a very limited sense, I much prefer the broader and deeper implications of self-control.

THE SPIRIT IS IN CONTROL

This sublime fruit of the Spirit is not negative. It does not consist of a list of what we are against or will not do.

Rather it consists of a very positive capacity to know who we are and what we will do because the Spirit is in control of our abilities and aptitudes, as well as our appetites. We can have power over ourselves only when we have submitted to the Spirit's control and power *in* us. Christ-control is the basis of self-control. Call central casting, the Lord Himself, for the real you.

Self-control is inseparably related to the fruit of gentleness. In the previous chapter we discovered that means living with the assurance that Christ is in us. Such an awareness results in the development of the special person each of us was created to be. It is very exciting to realize that our Lord has a strategy and plan for each of us.

We often think of personality as the irrevocable result of parental and environmental conditioning. A young man said to his father, "What I am is what you've made me. The ship has come in." That is to evade the opportunity and responsibility we all have to accept the Lord's reshaping of our personalities. He can affirm and strengthen what we are, in keeping with the uniqueness He has planned for us, and then He can reform anything that distorts or hinders our becoming all that we were meant to be.

When we yield our personalities to the Lord's scrutiny and renovation, He begins a magnificent transformation. That means surrendering our values, attitudes, actions, and reactions to Him. In profound times of prayer and meditation, we can talk to Him about the person we are in every dimension and relationship and then listen to Him as He tenderly shows us areas that need to be remolded to be more like Him.

THE HERO IN YOUR SOUL

The secret of discovering a truly unique personality is to focus on Christ. We become like our heroes, and He is the only reliable hero of our souls. In 1928, Arthur John Gossip entitled one of his books *The Hero in Thy Soul*—I like that! The better we know Christ, the more we concentrate on His message and life, and the closer we will come to being the special, distinct persons He intended. It is amazing. The deeper we grow in Christ, the more we become free to be our true selves. He does not put us into a straitjacket of sameness. Rather, He liberates us with new values, priorities, attitudes, and goals which begin to surface in our personalities. Human nature can be changed. We do not have to remain the people we are.

A few years ago, I experienced great physical reformation in intensive physiotherapy. In a series of ten sessions with a highly trained physiotherapist, my body underwent remarkable changes. Tightened tendons, conditioned by years of bad habits of posture were stretched and released. A hump in my back, formed by long hours slouched over my writing desk, was removed. Constricted muscles in my stomach that were pulling me down into a stooped posture were liberated so that I could stand up straight. Years of unhealthy self-conditioning of my body were reversed. Over the months of therapy, I grew an inch! I did not have to be the physical person I was for the rest of my life. My body was like plastic, and under the skilled hands of the therapist, I was liberated to stand, walk, and sit differently.

I have shared this personal experience as an illustration that none of us needs to remain the person we are. What that series of treatments did to my body, Christ has done and continues to do with my personality. I am not the personality I was; nor am I the person I will be. Seldom a day goes by without the Lord's impact. Ever since I yielded the control of my personality development to Him, He has been at work. He's not finished with me, nor will He ever be. In daily times with Him, He helps me look back over what I have been, said, and done. He always begins with what has been creative and good. Then, with masterful sensitivity, He penetrates into my relationships with myself and others. His questions are incisive. "Why did you feel it necessary to do or say that?" "What insecurity, defensiveness, or arrogance caused this?" "What would you have been like if you had been trusting Me and My guidance in that situation?" Following that is a remedial time of thinking with Him on how I can be more His person in the future.

FIVE *I*'S FOR DISCOVERING THE REAL *I*

The Lord offers us five *I*'s for discovering the real *I*. The first is **introspection.** That means daring to look inward to discover the roots of our personality. Why are we the people we are? What shaped our character? Whom are we trying to emulate? What is right and what is less than maximum?

The second step is **integration.** Christ takes inner control over our persons. When we put Him first in our lives, seek first His kingdom, and want what He wants for us, there is a new integration around His lordship. This is the control that liberates. Memories are sorted out, values are scrutinized, hopes are refashioned.

The third flows naturally. From integration comes **integrity.** We can dare to be outwardly what the Lord has enabled us to be inwardly. Integrity is the capacity to act in keeping with our beliefs and convictions—consistency! People around us will be able to say those seven dynamic words we all long to hear: "What you see is what you get." We all want to be people on whom others can depend in life's changes and challenges. We urgently desire to be the kind of parents, friends, and leaders whose attitudes and actions will be predictably consistent with the individual persons we really are.

Intuition is the fourth dimension. A life under Christ's control is gifted with an inner device that discerns what's right and does it. The Spirit's gifts of wisdom and discernment give us the X-ray vision we talked about earlier. It helps us to see beneath the surface of things. We are empowered to think clearly and feel sensitively about what is going on around us. Our minds and emotions become agents of the Spirit to guide us in times of pressure and opportunity.

I have a friend who has yielded to the Spirit's control so completely that he can penetrate deeply into problems and see the potential for advancement they offer. People around him are often heard to remark, "That guy sees and understands. How come his perception is so sharp?" The fruit of self-control as a result of Christ control is the only explanation. His faithfulness to daily prayer makes him an effective, intuitive leader. It is a supernatural gift. Without the indwelling Spirit, he would be as dull, insensitive, and unadventuresome as the people whom he constantly amazes.

The final "I" is **individuality.** We hear a lot of I've-got-to-be-me! individualism which is a poor facsimile for Christ-centered individuality. Individualism is a self-conscious effort to be different and distinct. It always calls attention to itself and must be fortified by disclaimers such as "Well, that's who I am. If you don't like it, that's your problem!" Individuality is inadvertent when the focus is on Christ and not on ourselves. We do not need to strive to be different. Christ is our difference. He makes us individuals who are free to live by grace and follow His guidance. The result will be people unlike anyone else, yet people who are concerned more about others than themselves.

The old statement, "God threw away the mold after he made him" is both true and untrue. Our mold is Christ and we come back to Him repeatedly for the clay of our personalities to be recast. The result will be freedom from self-consciousness or defensiveness.

In the context of all this, we can take another look at the word temperance as a translation of *egkrateia*. A tempered person has gone through the refining process. He or she has been hammered out on the anvil of the Lord's gracious, but persistent, reshaping. Then temperance is freedom from eccentric extremes and indulgences. The things which do not contribute to the Lord's best for us can be discarded or used without compulsion. Nothing that we eat or drink will be needed to fortify a depleted ego. Behavior patterns which trip us up in following Christ can be faced and surrendered to Him. All the things we consume or the distracting habits we form out of intemperance will be dislodged from their hold on us.

BALANCE IN A BEGUILING WORLD

There is a great word called *equipoise*. It means balance. When the inner power of Christ is balanced perfectly with the outward pressures of the world, that is equipoise. It is another way of describing self-control.

We live in such a beguiling world. As we are pulled in so many directions it is easy to allow our minds to drift into fantasies, our wills to make decisions inconsistent with the character of Christ, and our bodies to be engaged in practices which are not in keeping with His lordship.

Everything that was manifest in the character of Jesus of Nazareth is reproducible in you and me. "The Father and I will come and make our home in you," Christ said (John 14:23, paraphrase). It is a word of cheer and a word of challenge.

Paul gives the Galatians, and us, the secret of how to realize power over oneself. He says that we have crucified the flesh, and now as we live by the Spirit we should also walk by the Spirit. "The Spirit has given us life; He must also control our lives" (Galatians 5:25, TEV).

The term *flesh* is a kind of biblical shorthand for our humanity independent and separate from Jesus Christ. The exciting life begins when our minds, emotions, wills, and bodies are joyously surrendered to Christ's infinite control. That also includes every relationship of our lives. When we walk in the Spirit, Paul says, we will not fulfill the lusts of the flesh.

Do you remember when you took your first steps "in the Spirit"? Just as we learn to commit our weight to the ground step by step, in the same way we reach out to venture love and peace, patience and kindness—beyond our own hoarded resources, confident of the Spirit's limitless and ever-ready supply. Soon we will have acquired the greatest skill of all: walking in the Spirit.

For Christians battling the pull of the lower nature, Paul's code name *fruit* is an invitation to a radical transformation of the whole of human existence. Paul lists the "works of the flesh" in Galatians 5 and heralds the fruit of the Spirit as the antidote. For example, when we go around nursing giant-size hostilities, initiating quarrels, and constantly putting up opposite points of view, we are boycotting the Spirit's stores of gentleness and peace.

When we are fully in touch with who we are—the new person we are in Christ—an unmistakable outward radiance will reflect the splendor within. We have discovered the thermostatic control within that opens the channel to becoming the new breed of men and women we were intended to be. There is no way to hide it.

I'll never forget a wonderful period of uninterrupted time I had with my mother a few years before she died. Mother had sewn a new red dress for the occasion, spent the morning at the hairdresser, cleaned the house, had the coffee on the stove, and was all ready for my arrival.

We sat and talked like we had not talked for years, and like we might never talk again. She got out some of the old scrapbooks and albums, and entrusted to me a photo that is now one of my most cherished possessions. It was a picture of my father when he was my age. Years before she had put it away to give to me in such a moment. My eyes devoured the photo for marks of the heredity we shared. I traced the lines and contours in my father's face now evident in my own.

I trust the same kind of excitement has been in you as you have read these chapters. Have you been looking for and detecting the inescapable marks of an emerging family likeness to your own heredity? Paul's code name *fruit*, far from being archaic, is the flash of an eloquent symbol to remind us that all the graces and characteristics of God are to be modeled in the daily life and relationships of His children. *He wants to make us like His Son.*

Are we doing it? Are we giving the world a symmetrical, authentic, fully-formed image of Christ? There is still time. Spiritual growth is not a matter of chronology alone. It's a matter of your spirit. Of heart. Of who you are to the next person you meet. In the next crisis you face. In the next moment you live.

Central casting is calling. There is a need for someone to be the real you. Why not you? The magnificent vision of the amazing new you, as seen through the eyes of Christ, qualifies you to take the part.

ABOUT THE AUTHOR

IF YOU WERE TO ASK Lloyd Ogilvie what he does, his quick reply would be, "I'm a listener!" That may seem like an unusual response from a person who is known for his speaking and writing, but what Dr. Ogilvie has to say comes from attentive listening—to God and to people.

In addition to his pastoral counseling and extensive correspondence, each year he does a survey of what's on the minds and hearts of his congregation and his radio and television audiences. Then, in prayer and study, he listens to God for His answers in the Bible. This relational approach to communicating the gospel has made his messages on-target biblical expositions addressing the deepest concerns and most urgent questions of people. He has dedicated his life to the "exciting adventure of discipleship," and to communicating his discoveries to others in a vivid, practical, down-to-earth way. He combines a rich blend of scholarship and fresh inspiration with real-life illustrations, anecdotes, and stories about the great adventure of life in Christ.

Dr. Ogilvie is the Senior Pastor of the historic First Presbyterian Church of Hollywood. His radio and television ministry, *Let God Love You*, is broadcast throughout the nation. In 1988, he was named "Preacher of the Year" by the National Association of Religious Broadcasters.

He is the author of thirty books in which his readers are brought into the very presence of Jesus Christ, where they can experience the love, compassion, and healing power of the Lord. Dr. Ogilvie also serves as the General Editor of the *Communicator's Commentary*, a thirty-five volume exposition of the books of the Bible, and is a contributor to many magazines. His speaking engagements take him to conferences and retreats throughout the world.

As pastor of his church, Dr. Ogilvie leads a large staff of pastors and professional workers in equipping the members of the church for their ministry in the world. The church is distinguished for its healing ministry and its many task-force groups working to impact the major social problems of the Los Angeles area.

Dr. Ogilvie was educated at Lake Forrest College, Garrett Theological Seminary, and New College, University of Edinburgh. He holds doctoral degrees from Witworth College, Redlands University, Moravian Seminary, and Eastern College.

Step 1 # God's Purpose: Peace and Life

God loves you and wants you to experience peace and life—abundant and eternal.

The Bible Says . . .

"... we have peace with God through our Lord Jesus Christ." Romans 5:1

"For God so loved the world that He gave His only begotten Son, that whoever believes in Him should not perish but have everlasting life." John 3:16

"... I have come that they may have life, and that they may have it more abundantly." John 10:10b

Since God planned for us to have peace and the abundant life right now, why are most people not having this experience?

 Step 2 # Our Problem: Separation

God created us in His own image to have an abundant life. He did not make us as robots to automatically love and obey Him, but gave us a will and a freedom of choice.

We chose to disobey God and go our own willful way. We still make this choice today. This results in separation from God.

Our choice results in separation from God.

The Bible Says . . .

"For all have sinned and fall short of the glory of God." Romans 3:23

"For the wages of sin is death, but the gift of God is eternal life in Christ Jesus our Lord." Romans 6:23

People (Sinful)

God (Holy)

Our Attempts

Through the ages, individuals have tried in many ways to bridge this gap . . . without success . . .

The Bible Says . . .

"There is a way that seems right to man, but in the end it leads to death." Proverbs 14:12

"But your iniquities have separated you from God; and your sins have hidden His face from you, so that He will not hear." Isaiah 59:2

There is only one remedy for this problem of separation.

Step 3 # God's Remedy: The Cross

Jesus Christ is the only answer to this problem. He died on the Cross and rose from the grave, paying the penalty for our sin and bridging the gap between God and people.

The Bible Says . . .

". . . God is on one side and all the people on the other side, and Christ Jesus, Himself man, is between them to bring them together . . ." 1 Timothy 2:5

"For Christ also has suffered once for sins, the just for the unjust, that He might bring us to God . . ." 1 Peter 3:18a

"But God demonstrates His own love for us in this: While we were still sinners, Christ died for us." Romans 5:8

God has provided the only way . . . we must make the choice . . .

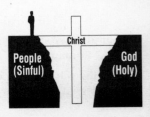

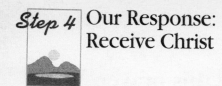 # Our Response: Receive Christ

We must trust Jesus Christ and receive Him by personal invitation.

The Bible Says . . .

"Behold, I stand at the door and knock. If anyone hears My voice and opens the door, I will come in to him and dine with him, and he with Me." Revelation 3:20

"But as many as received Him, to them He gave the right to become children of God, even to those who believe in His name." John 1:12

". . . if you confess with your mouth the Lord Jesus and believe in your heart that God has raised Him from the dead, you will be saved." Romans 10:9

Are you here . . . or here?

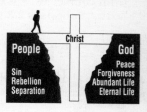

Is there any good reason why you cannot receive Jesus Christ right now?

How to receive Christ:

1. Admit your need (I am a sinner).
2. Be willing to turn from your sins (repent).
3. Believe that Jesus Christ died for you on the Cross and rose from the grave.
4. Through prayer, invite Jesus Christ to come in and control your life through the Holy Spirit. (Receive Him as Lord and Savior.)

What to Pray:

Dear Lord Jesus,

I know that I am a sinner and need Your forgiveness. I believe that You died for my sins. I want to turn from my sins. I now invite You to come into my heart and life. I want to trust and follow You as Lord and Savior.

In Jesus' name. Amen.

_____   _____
Date   Signature

God's Assurance: His Word

If you prayed this prayer,

The Bible Says...

"For 'whoever calls upon the name of the Lord will be saved.'"
Romans 10:13

Did you sincerely ask Jesus Christ to come into your life? Where is He right now? What has He given you?

"For it is by grace you have been saved, through faith—and this is not from yourselves, it is the gift of God—not by works, so that no one can boast." Ephesians 2:8,9

The Bible Says...

"He who has the Son has life; he who does not have the Son of God does not have life. These things I have written to you who believe in the name of the Son of God, that you may know that you have eternal life, and that you may continue to believe in the name of the Son of God." 1 John 5:12–13, NKJV

Receiving Christ, we are born into God's family through the supernatural work of the Holy Spirit who indwells every believer...this is called regeneration or the "new birth."

This is just the beginning of a wonderful new life in Christ. To deepen this relationship you should:

1. Read your Bible every day to know Christ better.
2. Talk to God in prayer every day.
3. Tell others about Christ.
4. Worship, fellowship, and serve with other Christians in a church where Christ is preached.
5. As Christ's representative in a needy world, demonstrate your new life by your love and concern for others.

God bless you as you do.

Billy Graham

If you want further help in the decision you have made, write to:
Billy Graham Evangelistic Association P.O. Box 779, Minneapolis, Minnesota 55440-0779